The Crystal and the Way of Light

D1501239

The Crystal and the Way of Light

Sutra, Tantra, and Dzogchen

by

Chögyal Namkhai Norbu

compiled and edited by

John Shane

Snow Lion
Boulder

Snow Lion
An imprint of Shambhala Publications, Inc.
2129 13th Street
Boulder, Colorado 80302
www.shambhala.com

First published in the United Kingdom by Penguin Books Ltd, 1986

IPC — 087EN00 — Approved by the International Publications
Committee on the Dzogchen Community founded by Chögyal
Namkhai Norbu.

13 12 11 10 9 8

Printed in the United States of America

Shambhala Publications makes every effort to print on acid-free, recy-
cled paper.

Snow Lion is distributed worldwide by Penguin Random House, Inc.,
and its subsidiaries.

Cataloging-in-Publication data is available from the Library of Congress.

Contents

Illustrations

Plates

Line drawings

This book is dedicated to my master, Changchub Dorje, and to my uncles Ogyen Tendzin and Khyentse Chökyi Wangchug, and to the benefit of all sentient beings.

—Namkhai Norbu

Editor's Note to the Snow Lion Edition

When, in 1980, I was first invited to work with Chögyal Namkhai Norbu to produce a book in English about Dzogchen, it was envisaged that the project would take about a year. But in the end the project took four years to complete, and *The Crystal and the Way of Light* was not, in fact, published until 1986. It is worth remembering, as Snow Lion Publications is preparing to release a new, revised and updated edition of *The Crystal* in the United States, that there were no books about Dzogchen available for the general Western reader at the time this book was first published. Furthermore, Chögyal Namkhai Norbu was practically the only Tibetan lama who was willing, at that time, to teach Westerners openly about Dzogchen. The extraordinary generosity of his attitude in relation to what was regarded in many circles as a reserved teaching was based on his great wisdom and clarity, as he clearly foresaw the enormous growth of interest in Tibetan Buddhism that would develop in the following years. He was fully aware that there was great hunger in the hearts of an increasing number of people for a teaching that they could practice in the midst of their busy lives in a world that seemed to be turning faster with every passing year, and he knew from his own experience that Dzogchen was a teaching ideally suited to their needs.

As it turned out, Rinpoche's intuition of the way things would develop was extremely accurate, and the interest in authentic spiritual teachings that was growing so fast in the West lead to *The Crystal* immediately being a great success in publishing terms. This surprising success seems particularly impressive when, with the benefit of hindsight, one considers that Tibet and Tibetan Buddhism were relatively obscure subjects at that time, and that the Dzogchen teachings themselves—which are the subject of this book—were not at all well-known even among those already interested in Buddhism. Now, of course, as we approach the turn of the century and the beginning of a new millennium, Tibet is a fashionable cause, and there are many books available on every aspect of Tibetan Buddhism, including Dzogchen, which is no longer an obscure subject known only to a few Tibetologists.

But the arrival of other books on the same subject seems not to have diminished the interest in *The Crystal and the Way of Light* that arose when it was first published: it has continued to find new readers, and we have been fortunate in that it has remained in print in various editions with a number of publishers over the years. This has been a source of great satisfaction both to Rinpoche and myself—as has the gradual process of seeing the book translated into more than a dozen different languages so far, including Czech, French, German, Italian, Polish, Russian (four separate Samizdat editions), Spanish—and more surprisingly perhaps, Mandarin Chinese.

The Crystal was originally compiled from the transcripts of tapes of oral teachings given by Chögyal Namkhai Norbu at retreats and lectures in various parts of the world between 1979 and 1986, as well as from notes that I myself made at lectures that were not 'officially' recorded. It also includes material arising from private conversations with Rinpoche that took place during the years that I travelled round the world with him, often acting as his translator.

Although Rinpoche had a good knowledge of English, he generally preferred, until late in 1984, to teach in Italian, the Western language with which he was at the time most familiar. He used to speak a few sentences in Italian and then pause to allow time for a translation to be made into the language of the majority of his listeners—whatever language that might be. When in Italy, of course, the majority of his listeners would not need a translation—but Rinpoche would still pause in his talks to allow time for a translation to be made into English for those present who did not understand Italian.

This book could not, then, have been produced without the dedicated effort of all those who, over the years, translated, recorded, and transcribed Rinpoche's teachings. But although the spontaneous translations made at the retreats were often inspired and the subsequent transcriptions of the talks were scrupulously faithful to what was recorded on the tapes, what actually appeared on the printed page of the transcripts left much to be desired in terms of both clarity of meaning and consistency of language.

One of the principal tasks of the editor was, then, to render all the material used in the book into good written English and to ensure a consistency of vocabulary and grammatical use that was lacking in the original transcripts.

But over and above that, from the many volumes of transcribed teachings dealing in detail with different topics, an overall structure had to be devised for the book that would reflect the inherent structure of the teachings as a whole, without losing the very distinctive quality of Rinpoche's oral teaching style. I attempted to do this by establishing in the book a pattern of alternating between the presentation of Rinpoche's teachings themselves and the entertaining and illuminating stories that Rinpoche so effectively uses to illustrate those teachings. This was exactly the way in which Rinpoche's individual talks were structured; it is hoped that this presentation will convey the extremely direct and personal quality of Rinpoche's teachings.

I mentioned above that the original book took four years to write instead of one, and the reason for this was that since I was never fully satisfied with the result, I kept on revising the manuscript over and over again. When I asked him for advice, Rinpoche suggested that I compile a book that my mother—an intelligent, educated and cultured woman who knew nothing about Buddhism—would understand and find useful. And that is what I tried to do.

When I first began working on this project I wanted to include everything that Rinpoche had taught, leaving nothing out, and this ambition led the first completed version of the book to be about five times as long as the version that was finally published. I gradually came to realize that what was needed was not a book that contained everything that Rinpoche had ever taught, but rather one that contained just enough of his teachings to give the reader exactly what he or she needed to know. So each time I rewrote the book after that realization, it got shorter and simpler, until it found its present form. Since the book was aimed at the general, as well as the scholarly reader, I tried as much as possible to avoid weighting the text down with too many footnotes, and I included a range of illustrations with the text to give the reader a real feeling for the art and culture of the Tibet while he or she absorbs the sometimes complex information contained in the written parts of the book.

If I succeeded to any extent in my work as editor, it was due to the extraordinary patience of Chögyal Namkhai Norbu himself, who continually made time available in private for further explanation and clarification. But any errors or wrong emphasis that may remain in the text are, of course, entirely my own responsibility.

Beyond the work of those who translated and transcribed Rinpoche's talks, many friends and colleagues helped with the text of the book and I would like to thank a few of them here by name. Brian Beresford (who has now, sadly, passed away), Jill Purce and Nancy Simmons, among many others, all made important contributions to the evolution of the original book.

In the preparation of this revised and updated edition for Snow Lion Publications, the advice and suggestions of my colleagues on the International Publishing Committee of the Dzogchen Community, Adriano Clemente and James Valby, have been invaluable, as have the comments of the many other translators who have translated the book into various languages over the years and who brought difficult areas of the book to my attention. Elias Capriles of Merida, Venezuela, the translator of *The Crystal* into Spanish, in particular, raised very many important points which have been incorporated into the text and footnotes of this new edition.

Authors and editors so commonly thank their life partners for their 'unfailing support and encouragement' that it becomes difficult to find words to thank my wife without sounding as if I am just reciting a stock formula. But my wife Jo really deserves something better than that. All the journeys around the world that I made with Rinpoche while writing this book were made together with her, and she was with me every step of the way throughout the four years in which I laboured over rewrite after rewrite, just as she has been there during the many weeks that it has taken to revise the manuscript once again for this new edition. I really can't imagine how I could have completed this project without her help.

Finally, and most importantly, I must, of course, express my gratitude to Rinpoche himself for inviting me to work with him on this book in the first place, and then for all his kindness and patience as the project took shape. Knowing as I do that I am just one person among all the very many students all over the world who make demands on his time and energy, it is a source of never-ending wonder to me that he is able to so compassionately offer us all his continuing guidance.

In the forward to the original edition, I wrote:

> At this time of pressing crisis for humanity, it is of the utmost importance that the ancient traditions of wisdom that lead to the transformation of the individual should be preserved and communicated clearly, as they have such a great contribution to offer to that peaceful transformation of society upon which the future survival of our species and our planet now depends. I hope that the collaboration with Chögyal Namkhai Norbu on this book, which it has been my great privilege to enjoy, will truly serve to play some part, however small, in the great endeavor of bringing strife and discord to an end, and in furthering peace and freedom from suffering for all beings.

Those words and the sentiments they express are as true now as they were at the time that I originally wrote them, and I am happy to conclude this introduction to the new edition of *The Crystal* by including them here.

I have done my best to make *The Crystal and the Way of Light* as faithful a representation of Rinpoche's teachings as I am able to do. But please remember that, in approaching the

Dzogchen teachings, no book can ever be a substitute for receiving transmission from a fully qualified master. May those who do not already have such a true 'spiritual friend' be fortunate enough to find one!

May it be auspicious!

John Shane
Night of the Full Moon, November 1999

The Six Vajra Verses

Although apparent phenomena
manifest as diversity
  yet this diversity is non-dual,
  and of all the multiplicity
  of individual things that exist
none can be confined in a limited concept.

Staying free from the trap of any attempt
to say it's 'like this', or 'like that',
it becomes clear that all manifested forms
are aspects of the infinite formless,
  and, indivisible from it,
  are self-perfected.

Seeing that everything is self-perfected
  from the very beginning,
the disease of striving for any achievement
  comes to an end of its own accord,
and just remaining in the natural state as it is,
the presence of non-dual contemplation
continuously, spontaneously arises.

The Six Vajra Verses, or more literally, the 'Six Vajra Lines', since the original Tibetan consists of only six lines, contain a perfect résumé of the Dzogchen teachings. This translation is by Brian Beresford and John Shane, in a fairly free rendering following the oral explanation of Chögyal Namkhai Norbu. The illustration below shows the Six Verses in Tibetan cursive *Umed* script; the calligraphy is by Chögyal Namkhai Norbu. The whole of the main text of this book could be considered to be a commentary on these Six Verses, which are the content of the *Trashipai Pal Rigpai Khujug Tantra*, the 'Fortune-Bringing Cuckoo of Non-dual

Awareness (*rigpa*) Tantra'. As the cuckoo is the first herald of coming spring, so this tantra and these verses are the heralds of coming spiritual awakening.

—*Calligraphy by Chögyal Namkhai Norbu*

Salutation to the Three Roots

Namo Guru Bhya!
Namo Deva Bhya!
Namo Dakini Bhya!

Homage to the Dzogchen Teachings

Just as the sun rises in the sky, so, too,
may the Great Secret Treasure of all the Victorious Ones,*
the supreme Dzogchen teaching, arise and spread in all realms!

—*Padmsambhava*

*The 'Victorious Ones' referred to are those who have overcome the dualistic condition.

The white Tibetan letter 'A', symbol of the primordial state

Chapter One

My Birth, Early Life, and Education; and How I Came to Meet My Principal Master

> From the very beginning
> all the infinite number of beings that exist
> have as their essential inherent condition
> the perfectly pure state of an enlightened being;
> knowing this to be true also of me,
> I commit myself to supreme realization.
>
> *Lines on Bodhicitta, written by Longchenpa (1308-63),*
> *expressing the concept of the Base in the Anuyoga*

When I was born, in the village of Geug, in the Kongra district of Derghe, eastern Tibet, in the tenth month of the year of the Earth Tiger (December 1938), it is said that the rose trees outside my parent's house bloomed even though it was winter. Two of my uncles came at once to visit my family. They had been disciples of a certain great master, Adzam Drugpa, who had died some years before, and they were both now Dzogchen masters themselves. They firmly believed that I was a reincarnation of their master, both because of things that he had said to them before he died, and because he had bequeathed certain special possessions to a son who he said would be born to my parents after his death. When I was two years old I was officially recognized as a reincarnation by a high trulku of the Nyingmapa[1] school, who made me a gift of some robes. I don't remember many of the details of what happened then, but I do know that after that I received an awful lot of presents!

Later, at the age of five, I was also recognized by the sixteenth Karmapa and by the Situ Rinpoche of that time as the mind incarnation of another great master, who was in turn the reincarnation of the founder of the modern state of Bhutan, and whose lineage had been the Dharmarajas, or Chögyals[2], the temporal and spiritual rulers of that state, up until the early twentieth century. As I grew up, I was thus to be given quite a few names and titles, many of which are very long and grand sounding. But I have never used them, because I have always preferred the name my parents gave me at birth. They called me Namkhai Norbu, which is rather a special name in its own way. *Norbu* means jewel, and *Namkhai* means of the sky, or of space. It's unusual for the genitive to be used in Tibetan names, but that's what my parents chose to call me because, although they had four fine daughters, they had been longing for years to have a son.

So strong had been this longing, in fact, that they had engaged the services of a monk to perform an invocation of Tara [see illustration on p. 22] on their behalf for a whole year, asking for the granting of their wish. This monk also became my sister's tutor. Eventually, he had a dream which he interpreted as a

An eighteenth-century crystal polyhedron from Tibet (John Dugger and David Medalla, London)

favorable sign. He dreamed that a beautiful plant grew up right in front of the hearth of my parent's home. The plant put forth a beautiful yellow flower that opened and grew very big. The monk was sure that this indicated the birth of a male child. Later, when I was born, my parents were so happy that they felt I was a gift from the heavens. So they called me 'Jewel of Space', and that is the name I have always stuck to.

My parents were always very kind to me, and I grew up into a little boy as mischievous as any other, and learned to read and write at home. As a young child, I often dreamed I was travelling at great speed inside what seemed to me to be a tiger, a strange roaring beast. I had never seen a motor vehicle, as there were none at that time in our part of Tibet. Later, of course, I came to travel in many cars, and then I recognized them as being what I had seen in my dreams. When, as a teenager, I did catch my first sight of a lorry, I was on horseback on a mountain side at night looking down at the vehicles passing on the new Chinese road below.

The tail lights glowed red on the giant trucks thundering by, and I thought they must be on fire. I also dreamed of strange flaming flying objects that exploded causing terrible destruction. I now know that what I saw were the missiles that were being developed far away in other parts of the world.

I sometimes played such pranks on our neighbors that I would be in serious trouble when my father came home from the travels that his work often involved. He would beat me, and I would be very angry, and try to retaliate against the neighbors who had told my father what I had done by playing even more pranks on them. Then, of course, I would be in more trouble again. I began to become more considerate largely as a result of my grandmother's influence. She had been a disciple of Adzam Drugpa, and she took a great interest in me. She sometimes managed to keep me from being punished by preventing my parents finding out what I had done. I remember that I once found the dead body of a large rodent called a marmot. Unnoticed by anyone I spent a blissful afternoon playing with the dead creature, even filling the body up with water and whirling it round my head. But when I

Green Tara. There are twenty-one different Sambhogakaya manifestations of Tara, a feminine emanation of the primordial Dharmakaya Buddha Amitabha. Each form of Tara embodies a particular aspect of compassion. Green Tara represents the active, energic aspect of compassion, and she is the national protectress of Tibet, while White Tara, for example, embodies the fertile, motherly aspect of compassion. (Line drawing by Nigel Wellings.)

took my plaything to bed with me my grandmother noticed it. She knew that my mother would have been very upset if she had known what I had been doing, and would have worried that I might become infected with some disease, so my grandmother didn't tell anyone. I thought this was very kind of her, and in fact I loved her very much. So when I saw her quietly weeping to herself about my behavior when she thought I was asleep, I was deeply moved, and resolved to mend my ways. But I can't say that I ever completely succeeded in overcoming my mischievousness altogether.

When I was five years old, I was playing outside our house one day when twelve monks arrived, all very elegantly dressed. The place where we lived was very isolated, and hardly any travellers ever passed, so I was very surprised to see them. I couldn't think why they had come. They went into the house, and a little later I was called to go in after them. I was taken into the small shrine room we had there, and they dressed me in fine silk robes. I didn't understand why I was being dressed up, but I enjoyed it just the same. I sat there, on a high throne they had specially prepared for me, for hours and hours while they performed a ritual, and then they went away. I thought to myself, 'Well, that's the end of that'. But everyone went on reminding me that I was a reincarnation and showing me great respect, and I soon realized that far from being the end of anything, everything was just beginning.

A couple of weeks later some monks came and took me to Derghe Gönchen monastery, which was a very important place in that region: the King of Derghe himself lived there. My father worked in the King's administration, at first as an official roughly equivalent to a mayor or provincial governor in the West, and later, since he loved animals so much, as the head of a department whose function was to prevent hunting out of season or in excess in the whole of that part of Tibet. I was taken in to see the King, and since I was now recognized as a reincarnation, he put an entire building inside the monastery compound at my disposal. I lived there until I was nine years old with a master, a teacher who made me study hard day and night. There were many things to learn, including all the rules and prayers of the monastery. A monk normally finishes at nineteen years of age the phase of study I undertook there, but I completed it at the age of eight, because my master was so strict, and I was allowed no free time at all. I also had a natural gift for memorizing things.

My mischievous side did manage to surface from time to time, however. I remember, for example, that once when the King was involved in a military ceremony that required him to sit still on horseback for a long time in the courtyard below and opposite the first floor window of my house, I leaned over the sill and used a mirror to reflect the sun's rays into his eyes to dazzle him. My intention, innocent enough, was to lighten the rather overly heavy seriousness of the occasion for the King, and fortunately for me he knew me very well by that time, so that, instead of being offended, he even enjoyed the joke himself, once he had recovered his composure.

Then for a year I learned all the rules for the drawing and practice of mandala, after which I went away to monastic college. A college always has its rules and regulations, and the normal curriculum of the one I attended was that one studied there for five years. But since I entered at a much earlier age than usual, I was there for six years. The normal age of entry was at least thirteen, and I was only nine years old when I went there, so they didn't count my first year which was regarded as a sort of trial period to see if I was capable of staying the course. It wasn't just a matter of memorizing things any longer: we studied philosophy, which requires a capacity to reason well, and many people found the going too tough and dropped out.

Being so much younger than all the other students, life in the college certainly wasn't always easy for me either, and I suffered as others do from the rigors of life in that kind of institution. I had to learn some practical lessons very quickly. When my father took me to the college for my first term, he left with me enough supplies for the whole three months that would have to pass before I would go home again for a holiday. But I'd never had to manage my provisions on my own before, and by about half way through the period they were supposed to last I had used up all my supplies because I was far too generous in my hospitality to all my new colleagues. When I had no food of my own left I managed to survive for about a week on the salty yak butter tea that was the only thing provided by the college, but then I got too hungry for my pride to matter any more, and I finally found the courage to face the humiliation of having to go to ask my teacher for help. He very kindly arranged for me to receive a bowl of soup every evening, and, of course, the next term I was a good deal more provident with my resources.

The regulations in the college were very strictly enforced, and we had to remain in our small rooms every evening to practice and study after dinner until bedtime. Butter lamps and coal for heating were supplied for our use, but not in very generous quantities, and I remember that once the butter in my lamp ran out before I had completed reading through the large number of practices I had to recite every night to maintain the commitments I had made in receiving the very many initiations given to a trulku like myself.

We weren't allowed to leave our rooms at that hour and there was a monk patrolling the corridors to make sure the rules were observed, so I didn't dare to go and ask a neighbor if I could borrow a lamp, but tried to read my practices by the light of the coal fire. I knew some of the texts well enough to be able to just about manage to recite them even when the embers had burned down to a mere glimmer, but when the last spark finally had gone out, there I was in the dark with a pile of long Tibetan pages still to be read if I was to maintain my samaya commitments. I didn't understand at that time how to maintain commitment by applying the essentials of the practice, and I interpreted and carried out all the instructions that were given to me by my teachers in a very literal manner.

In my holidays I found time to visit my two uncles and those visits were very important to me, because they were both practitioners of Dzogchen. One of these uncles was an abbot and the other a yogi, and in the course of later chapters of this book

I intend to tell some stories of my experiences with them that I hope will bring the Dzogchen teachings to life for the reader. My relationships with them were of very great importance to me throughout my college years, and their example as practitioners was a vital counterbalance to the emphasis on intellectual studies that dominated my life between the ages of nine and sixteen.

Finally, in 1954, at the age of sixteen, I completed my studies and left college. By then I knew a great deal about all the various forms of the teaching and was considered to be well educated about Tibetan medicine and astrology, too. I'd studied diligently with many masters, some of whom even considered that I had mastered the subject matter they had taught me sufficiently for them to have asked me to teach others in the college. I could recite whole texts of philosophy and ritual by heart, and so, as I graduated, I really believed that I'd learned a great deal. It wasn't until later that I came to realize that I hadn't really understood anything at all.

Though I did not yet know it, events were moving me towards the one particular master who was to bring all I had learned and experienced into a new and more profound perspective, and through contact with whom I was to come to a reawakening, and to a true understanding of the Dzogchen teachings. Through his inspiration I came to know the importance of these teachings, and eventually to teach them myself in the Western world. This master was not a grand personage. Tibetans in general are used to seeing the teachings represented by famous teachers of high rank, who present themselves in grand style. Without such outer signs, in fact, people usually can't recognize the qualities of a master, and I myself might have been no different.

But, on leaving college, I was given my first official responsibilities, and was sent to China as representative of Tibetan youth at the Provincial Assembly of the Province of Szechuan, the local governing body, and while I was there I began learning the Chinese language, and also taught Tibetan. So with these secondary activities as well as my official job, I was very busy. But I couldn't avoid noticing how very different the social and political structure was there, or keep from wondering how what was happening in China would eventually affect my own country and its people.

Then one night I had a dream—a particularly important dream—in which I saw a place with many white houses built of cement. Since this is not a Tibetan style of building, but is a type of construction commonly found in China, I mistakenly (as I later learned) assumed that these houses were Chinese. But when, while still dreaming, I moved closer to the buildings, I saw that the mantra of Padmasambhava was written in very large Tibetan script on one of them. I was amazed, because if this really was a Chinese house, why would there be a mantra written in Tibetan over the doorway?

So I opened the door, and went in, and inside I saw an old man—just a seemingly normal old man. But for whatever reason the question arose spontaneously in me: 'Could this man really be a master?' And to my surprise the old man bent to touch his forehead to mine in the way that Tibetan masters greet other masters, and he began to recite the mantra of Padmasambhava, which seemed to answer my question. What was happening still seemed very surprising to me, but I was by now fully convinced that the old man in my dream was a master.

Then he told me to go round to the other side of a large rock that was nearby, adding that in the middle of the rock I would find a cave containing eight natural mandalas. He told me to go there at once to look at them. This amazed me even more than just finding a master in such strange circumstances, but I nevertheless did as he said, and went right away to find the big rock that he had mentioned. Then, when I got to the cave in the rock, my father appeared behind me, and as I went into the cave, he began to recite the *Heart Sutra*, or *Prajnaparamita Hridaya*, an important Mahayana sutra, in a loud voice. I began to recite the sutra along with him, and together we walked all around inside the cave. Try as I could, I couldn't see the whole of the eight mandalas the master had told me to look for. I could only make out the corners and edges of them, but with their presence in my mind I awoke.

A year after this dream, when I had returned to Tibet from China, a man came to visit my father in our village, and I overheard him telling my father about an extraordinary doctor he'd just met. He described the place where the doctor lived, and he described the man himself in detail, and as he spoke the memory of my dream returned to me. I felt sure that the man he was describing was the same man I had seen in my dream.

I spoke to my father about this at once. I'd already told him about the dream I'd had in China of an old man who seemed to be a master, and now I reminded him of the dream, asking him if we could visit this doctor his friend was telling him about. My father agreed, and we set out the next day. We had to travel for four days on horseback, but when we got to the village where the doctor lived, the old man I met there really seemed to be the one I had seen in my dream. I really had the sense that I had been in that village before, with its Tibetan houses made in Chinese-style concrete. And the mantra was inscribed over the old man's door in exactly the same way I had seen in my dream.

All this meant that I had no doubt that this old man was to be my master, and right away on my first visit to his village, I became determined to remain there to receive teachings from him. His name was Changchub Dorje, and in terms of outward appearance he seemed like a normal country person of Tibet. His style of dress and his way of life were just completely normal on the surface. But as I shall relate later in this book, his state of being was far from ordinary.

The disciples who lived around him also lived their lives in a very ordinary way. Most of them were very simple people, not at all well-to-do, and they grew and tended crops, working the land and practicing together.

Changchub Dorje was a Dzogchen master, and Dzogchen does not depend on externals; rather it is a teaching about the essentials of the human condition.

And so, when I later came to leave Tibet because of the political difficulties there and finally settled in the West to take up a post as a Professor at the Oriental Institute in Naples, Italy,

I came to see that although the outer conditions and culture in which people lived were very different from those I had left behind in Tibet, the fundamental condition of every individual was no different.

I saw that since the Dzogchen teachings are not dependent on culture, they can be taught, understood, and practiced in any cultural context.

Chapter Two

An Introductory Perspective: The Dzogchen Teachings and the Culture of Tibet

> If you give an explanation of Dzogchen
> to a hundred people who are interested,
> this is not enough;
> but if you give an explanation
> to one person who is not interested,
> this is too much.
>
> —*Garab Dorje*

Many people today are not interested at all in spiritual matters, and their lack of interest is reinforced by the generally materialistic outlook of our society. If you ask them what they believe in, they may even say that they don't believe in anything. Such people think that all religion is based on faith, which they regard as little better than superstition, with no relevance to the modern world. But Dzogchen shouldn't be regarded as a religion, and it doesn't ask anyone to believe in anything. On the contrary, it suggests that the individual observe him or herself and discover for themselves what their actual condition is.

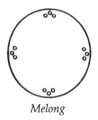

Melong

In the Dzogchen teachings, the individual is regarded as functioning at three interdependent levels, of body, voice or energy, and mind. Even someone who says they don't believe in anything cannot say they don't believe in their own body! It's basic to their existence, and the limits and problems of the body are clearly tangible. We feel cold and hunger, we suffer pain and loneliness, and we spend much of our lives in an attempt to overcome our physical suffering.

The level of energy, or voice, is not so easy to see, and not so widely understood. Even medical doctors in the West are largely ignorant of it, trying to cure all illnesses at a purely material level. But if the energy of an individual is disturbed, neither the body nor the mind of the individual will be well balanced. Certain illnesses, such as cancer, are caused by disturbances of the energy, and cannot be cured simply by surgery or medication. Similarly, many mental illnesses, and also some less severe mental problems, are caused by poor circulation of energy. Our minds are generally very complicated and confused, and even when we want to stay calm, we may find we can't, because our nervous and agitated energy won't allow us to.

So to deal with these problems of body, voice, and mind, the Dzogchen teachings present practices that work with each of these three levels of the individual, practices that can be integrated with the individual's daily life and which can thus change our whole life experience from one of tension and confusion to one of wisdom and true freedom. The teachings are not merely theoretical, they are practical; and though the Dzogchen teachings are extremely ancient, because the nature of the body, voice, and mind of the individual has not changed, these teachings remain as relevant to the human situation of today as they were to that of yesterday.

The Primordial State

The teaching of Dzogchen is in essence a teaching concerning the primordial state that is each individual's own intrinsic nature from the very beginning. To enter this state is to experience oneself as one is, as the center of the universe though not in the ordinary ego sense. The ordinary ego-centered consciousness is precisely the limited cage of dualistic vision that closes off the experience of one's own true nature, which is the space of the primordial state. To discover this primordial state is to understand the teaching of Dzogchen, and the function of the transmission of the teaching of Dzogchen is to communicate this state from one who has realized, or become established in it, to those who remain caught up in the dualistic condition. Even the name *Dzogchen*, which means 'Great Perfection', refers to the self-perfectedness of this state, fundamentally pure from the beginning, with nothing to reject or accept.

To understand and enter the primordial state one does not need intellectual, cultural, or historical knowledge. It is beyond intellect by its very nature. Yet when people encounter a teaching they have not heard of before, one of the first things they may want to know is where this teaching arose, where it came from, who taught it, and so on. This is understandable, but Dzogchen itself cannot be said to belong to the culture of any country. There is a tantra of Dzogchen, the *Dra Thalgyur Tsawai Gyüd*, for example, that says that the Dzogchen teaching can be found in thirteen solar systems other than our own, so we can't even truly say that the Dzogchen teaching belongs to this planet Earth, much less to any particular national culture. Although it is true that the tradition of Dzogchen that we are about to consider has been transmitted through the culture of Tibet that has harbored it ever since the beginning of recorded history in Tibet, we nevertheless cannot finally say that Dzogchen is Tibetan, because the primordial state itself has no nationality and is omnipresent.

But it is also true that beings everywhere have entered into the dualistic vision that veils the experience of the primordial state. And when realized beings have tried to communicate with them, they have only rarely been able to communicate the primordial state completely without words or symbols, so they have made use of whatever culture they found present, as a means of communication. In this way it has often happened that the culture and the teachings have become interwoven, and in the case of Tibet this is true to the extent that it is not possible to understand the culture without an understanding of the teachings.

It's not that the teachings of Dzogchen were ever particularly widespread or well-known in Tibet; in fact rather the reverse was true. Dzogchen was always a somewhat reserved teaching. But the Dzogchen teachings are the essence of all Tibetan teachings, so direct that they were always kept a little hidden, and people were often a little afraid of them. Furthermore, there existed a tradition of Dzogchen among the ancient Bön[1] traditions, the indigenous and largely shamanic traditions of Tibet, that pre-date the arrival of Buddhism from India.

Thus, if we consider the Dzogchen teachings as being the essence of all the Tibetan spiritual traditions, both Buddhist and Bön (though itself actually belonging to neither Buddhism nor Bön), and if we understand that the spiritual traditions of Tibet were the essence of Tibetan culture, then we can use the Dzogchen teachings as a key to the understanding of Tibetan culture as a whole. And with this perspective it can be seen how all the various aspects of Tibetan culture have been manifested as facets of the unified vision of realized beings, the masters of the spiritual traditions.

Like a crystal at the heart of the culture, the clarity of the primordial state, as manifested in the minds of many masters, has radiated the forms of Tibetan art and iconography, medicine, and astrology, like brilliant rays, or sparkling reflections. So by coming to understand the nature of the crystal, we will be better able to make sense of the rays and reflections that emanate from it.

Chapter Three

How My Master Changchub Dorje Showed Me the Real Meaning of Direct Introduction

> Knowledge of Dzogchen is like
> being on the highest mountain peak;
> no level of mountain remains mysterious or hidden,
> and whoever finds themselves on this highest peak
> cannot be conditioned by anyone or anything.
>
> *—from a tantra of the Dzogchen Upadesha*

When I went to my master Changchub Dorje, I was educated up to the hilt in the intellectual sense. My mind was filled with everything I'd learned in the monastic colleges. I thought that to receive transmission of the teachings, elaborate ritual initiations were essential and I asked Changchub Dorje to give me a certain initiation. I asked him every day for days and days, but he always refused.

'What's the use?' he'd say. 'You've already received so many of those initiations from your other masters; initiations like that

Double Vajra

are not the principle of the Dzogchen teachings. Transmission isn't only received in formal initiations.'

But no matter what he said, I remained fixed on the kind of perfectly performed ritual initiations other masters had always given me. I wasn't satisfied with his replies, and I wanted him to put on a special hat, prepare a mandala, and pour a little water on my head, or something like that. That was what I really, sincerely wanted; but he always continued to refuse.

Finally, I insisted so much that he at last agreed. He promised that about two months later, on the day of Padmasambhava, the tenth day of the Tibetan lunar month[1], he would give me the initiation I wanted, the empowerment of Samantabhadra and the peaceful and wrathful divinities of the Bardo[2]. This initiation is actually not very complicated, and a master skilled in such things could have completed it very quickly. But Changchub Dorje had never received a formal education, and he was not used to giving initiations. When the long-awaited day finally came, the initiation took him from about nine in the morning till midnight. To begin with, he had to prepare himself by performing a rite of self-initiation. This took him until mid-day to complete. Then he began the initiation for me. But, not being formally educated, not only couldn't he read the text himself, but on top of that I could see that he didn't know how to do all the ritual things he was supposed to do. He wasn't that kind of a master.

So Changchub Dorje had a disciple present as an assistant who was himself an expert teacher, and it was he who prepared all the mandalas and ritual objects. Then this disciple began to read the text to tell the master what he had to do next. But when he read out that a certain mudra, or gesture, should be done by the master giving the initiation, Changchub Dorje didn't know how to do it, so they had to stop while he learned it.

Then there was a whole long invocation that was supposed to be chanted, invoking all the masters of the lineage, and while chanting it, the master is supposed to sound a bell and a damaru, or small drum. Someone who is used to rituals can perform all this very quickly, but Changchub Dorje wasn't used to such things, and the whole situation became outrageous, a complete farce.

First of all he worked out with his assistant what was written in the notes to the text. 'Ah!' he said. 'It says here that you have to sound the bell!' So he took the bell, and for about five minutes all he did was sound it over and over again. Then it was read out to him that you have to sound the damaru. So he sounded the little drum over and over for about another five minutes. Then he suddenly said: 'Oh, now I see! You have to sound the bell and damaru together!' So he did that. But by then he had forgotten what it was that he was supposed to chant, so he had to go through it all again with the help of the disciple who could read.

Changchub Dorje himself hadn't had the kind of education that involves study, but was a practitioner who had manifested wisdom and clarity through the development of his practice, and it was because of this wisdom and clarity that he was considered to be a master. So he hadn't received the kind of monastic training that would have prepared him to give all the various kinds of formal empowerment, and he stumbled through the initiation he gave me taking all day and a good deal of the evening to do it. By the time he had finished, I was almost in a state of shock, as, given my own background, I knew very well how an initiation should be done, and it was nothing like this.

But by then it was nearly midnight, and we were all very hungry. We sang the *Song of the Vajra* [see p. 91] together many times. This is a short, slow, anthemic chant, characteristic of the way Dzogchen works with ritual, that leads the practitioner into contemplation through integration with its actual sound, the structure of its syllables and melody ensuring deep, relaxed breathing. Then we recited a short Gana Puja offering, and we ate.

After the meal the master gave me a real explanation of the true meaning of initiation and transmission, and I realized that despite all the formal initiations I had received at my college, I had never understood or entered into the true meaning of them.

Then, without interruption, for about three or four hours, Changchub Dorje gave me a real explanation of Dzogchen, not teaching me in an intellectual style, but talking to me in a very straightforward and relaxed, friendly, conversational way. Despite all my education, this was the first time a master had really made such a direct attempt to get me to understand something. What he said, and the way that he said it, was exactly like a tantra of Dzogchen, spoken spontaneously, continuously aloud, and I knew that even a very learned scholar would not be able to speak like that. Changchub Dorje was speaking from clarity and not just from an intellectual understanding.

From that day on I understood that intellectual study, which had always previously been so important to me, is only of secondary value. And I understood that the principle of transmission is not just the performance of rituals or initiations, or the giving of intellectual explanations. That day my mental constructions completely collapsed. Up until then I was completely boxed in with all the ideas I had received in my college education.

Transmission is vital to the introduction received in Dzogchen, and the Direct Introduction I received from Changchub Dorje that day, and continued to receive throughout my stay with him, was typical of the way in which transmission of the Dzogchen teachings has been passed on down the lineage from master to disciple, from the time of Garab Dorje, the first master of Dzogchen, who himself received transmission through direct visionary contact with the Sambhogakaya [see p. 162].

Although centuries before the time of Garab Dorje a simpler and less sophisticated form of the Dzogchen teachings had been introduced into the many streams of the Bön tradition by Shenrab Miwo, refer to drawing on facing page, the great reformer of Bön, nevertheless what we now know as the Three Series of the Dzogchen teachings were taught for the first time on this planet in this time cycle by Garab Dorje. And although the great master Padmasambhava, who came later, is undoubtedly more widely known, it was from Garab Dorje that he received transmission,

ག༤ེན་རབ་མེ་འོ་ཀུན་ལས་རྣམ་པ་རྒྱལ།

Tibetan wood-block print of Shenrab Miwo, seated on a lotus throne, holding a swastika scepter, Bön equivalent of the Buddhist vajra, or dorje, symbol of the indestructible, eternal nature of primordial energy. The earliest available historical records relate that a great Bön spiritual master, Shenrab Miwo, born in 1856 B.C.E., reformed and synthesized the various existing Bön traditions, replacing actual animal sacrifices with the use of ritual statuettes, and introducing the earliest known form of Dzogchen teaching (Yandagbai Sembön), a form less sophisticated than the Three Series of Garab Dorje. (Artist unknown.)

both directly, in the form of a visionary transmission across time and space, and in the usual way, as the teachings had descended down the lineage of Garab Dorje's disciples and their disciples in turn.

Garab Dorje was a totally realized being who manifested a birth in a Nirmanakaya form [see p. 163], as a human being, in the third century B.C.E., in the country of Ogyen, which was situated to the north west of India. He spent his life there teaching to both human beings and the dakinis [see Appendix 3 (commentary to plate 5)]. His final teaching before he entered the Body of Light was to summarize the teachings in Three Principles, sometimes known as The Three Last Statements of Garab Dorje.

The Life of Garab Dorje

Garab Dorje, unlike Buddha Shakyamuni, who lived before his time, but like Padmasambhava, who was to come later, did not manifest an ordinary birth. A realized being can choose the manner, time and place of his or her birth in a way that seems impossible from the limited point of view of dualistic vision. Garab Dorje's mother, Sudharma, was the daughter of the King of Ogyen, and she was a nun. The child she bore was conceived after a meditative vision, an event that both delighted and baffled her. She was ashamed and afraid that people would think badly of her or believe that the child was a phantom because he had been born to a virgin. So she hid him in a cinder pit.

But when, a few days later, she returned full of remorse to look for the child, she found him radiant and healthy, playing in the ashes where she had left him. It was then accepted by the court that the child was a miraculous incarnation of a great teacher and he was brought up in the King's palace. Spontaneously and untaught, out of his great clarity, he began to recite essential tantras as if from memory, and the King found such joy in his company that he named him Praharsha Vajra, which means Joyous Vajra in the language of Ogyen, a language similar to Sanskrit. In Tibetan that name becomes Garab Dorje.

At the age of seven, when all the learned pandits of the kingdom were gathered in debate, Garab Dorje defeated them in argument, showing far greater understanding than any of them. He then taught them the Dzogchen teachings, and the news rapidly spread far afield that a young boy considered to be the reincarnation of a great being living in the country of Ogyen was giving a teaching beyond the law of cause and effect. When the news reached India it greatly disturbed the Buddhist pandits there, and it was decided that the most learned pandit of all, whose name was Manjushrimitra and who was extremely skilled in logic and argument, should lead a party to defeat this impudent young upstart in debate. But when Manjushrimitra arrived, he found that the boy was indeed a great teacher and that he could not fault his teaching. It became clear to him that the child's realization went well beyond his own intellectual understanding. He then became deeply repentant, and confessed to Garab Dorje the wrong motivation he had had in coming to see him with the sole intention of debating with him and defeating him in argument. Garab Dorje forgave him, and proceeded to give him more teaching. What he did ask of Manjushrimitra, however, was that he, the greatest of all the Buddhist scholars of his time, should write a text setting out the argument of the teaching with which Garab Dorje had defeated him. The text that Manjushrimitra then wrote exists to the present day.[3]

To understand in what sense the teaching of Garab Dorje can be said to be beyond the fundamental law of karma, the law of cause and effect, and thus apparently contradictory to the teaching of the Buddha, and yet nevertheless still be a perfect teaching, we must consider the famous *Heart Sutra*, the essential summary of the vast Prajnaparamita sutras. This sutra proclaims the teaching on the nature of Shunyata, voidness, or emptiness of self-nature (the absence of inherent, independent existence posited by Buddhism), listing all the constituent elements with which we construct our reality, and stating that each in turn is void or empty (of self-nature). Thus the sutra expounds the voidness of the sense functions and their objects, repeating the formula: '... and so, because all phenomena are in essence void

Garab Dorje (Line drawing by Nigel Wellings.)

of self-nature, the eye cannot be said to have any independent existence, and similarly there is in reality no such "thing" as an ear, or a nose ... nor a faculty of seeing, nor of hearing, nor of smelling ...,' and so on. Then the text negates in the same way the supposed self-existence of all the central elements of the Buddha's teachings with a view to showing their essential voidness, including in this list of negations the statement that there is no karma, no law of cause and effect.

Since it is recorded in the sutra that the great bodhisattva[4] Avalokiteshvara was requested by the Buddha himself to give this teaching to the great arhat Shariputra, in front of an assembled multitude of all kinds of beings, and since, at the end of the sutra, the Buddha greatly praises the wisdom of Avalokiteshvara's words, and it is recorded that the whole company rejoiced, it is clear that there is a teaching beyond cause and effect, and indeed beyond all limits, right at the heart of the Buddha's teachings themselves.

Garab Dorje had many disciples both among human beings and among the dakinis, and continued to teach for the rest of his life. Finally, before he dissolved his body into the essence of the elements and entered into the realization of the Body of Light, he left the summary of his teachings known as his Three Principles, which were presented above.

The Three Principles of Garab Dorje, the Three Series of the Dzogchen Teachings, and Further Groups of Three

The Dzogchen teachings, though their aim is not to develop the intellect, but to bring one beyond the intellect into the primordial state, contain a precise and crystalline structure of interlinked explanations. The Three Principles of Garab Dorje are the essentials of this crystalline structure, and all the various aspects of the teaching can be seen to be linked to them, in a network of interlocking components of explanation, grouped in threes. Appenix 1 shows the correspondences between these groups of three.

The first of the Three Principles of Garab Dorje is Direct Introduction, the direct transmission of the primordial state from the master to the disciple. It should be clear that this transmission itself is not something that comes within the realm of the intellect. But there are three ways in which the Introduction can be presented: direct, symbolic, and oral. And these three styles of presentation are fundamental characteristics of what are known as the Three Series of Dzogchen teachings: the Mennagde, or Essential Series; the Longde or Series of Space; and the Semde, or Series of the Nature of the Mind. A diagram of these Three Series is also included in Appendix 1, which shows the particular approach of each. The Three Series should not be seen as three grades, or divisions, or a school. They are three modes of the presentation of Introduction, and three methods of practice, but they all aim to bring the practitioner to contemplation, and they are all equally Dzogchen teachings. The division of Garab Dorje's teaching into Three Series was carried out by Manjushrimitra, Garab Dorje's principal disciple, and continued by later masters.

The Mennagde works most specifically on the principle of Direct Introduction (being the Essential Series), while the Longde is more closely associated with symbolic introduction, and the Semde with oral introduction. So each Series has its particular way of presenting the introduction to contemplation and the primordial state, yet the same state is transmitted directly as an integral part of each Series. One can say that the Semde is really the fundamental basis for the transmission of the Dzogchen teachings, while the Longde works with the principal points of the Semde; and the Mennagde can be said to be the essential points of the Semde and the Longde, condensed by masters according to their experience and according to their discovery of terma[5] (or hidden treasures). But the Semde has tended to become rather overshadowed by the presentation of the Mennagde and at various times it has been necessary to reemphasize its importance.

Chapter Four

Dzogchen in Relation to the Various Levels of the Buddhist Path

> Give up all negative actions;
> always act perfectly in virtue;
> develop complete mastery of your own mind:
> this is the teaching of the Buddha.
>
> —*Buddha Shakyamuni*

> If thoughts arise, remain present in that state;
> if no thoughts arise, remain present in that state;
> there is no difference in the presence in either state.
>
> —*Garab Dorje*

The problem of dualism

It will be helpful in coming to an understanding of Dzogchen to consider it in relation to the various other spiritual paths within the spectrum of Buddhism in general, which are all equally precious, and have been taught for the benefit of beings of different levels of capacity. These paths all have the common aim of seeking to overcome the problem that arose when the individual entered into dualism, developing a spurious 'subjective self' or 'ego' that experiences the world as separate from itself, external and objective, and which continually tries to manipulate that world in order to obtain satisfaction and security. In truth, one will never manage to attain satisfaction and security this way, because the cause of suffering and dissatisfaction is none other than the fundamental sense of incompleteness that is the

Buddha Shakyamuni, the historical Buddha. (Line drawing by Nigel Wellings.)

inevitable consequence of being in the state of dualism—and, moreover, all the seemingly external phenomena on which we try to base our satisfaction and security are impermanent.

The Buddha was a totally realized being who manifested a human birth in India in the fifth century B.C.E. in order to be able to teach other human beings by means of his words and the example of his life. Suffering is something very concrete, which everyone knows and wants to avoid if possible, and the Buddha therefore began his teaching by talking about it in his famous formulation of the Four Noble Truths.

The first truth draws our attention to the fact that we suffer, pointing out the existence of the basic dissatisfaction inherent in our condition; the second truth explains the cause of dissatisfaction, which is the dualistic state and the unquenchable thirst (or desire) inherent in it: the subject reifies its objects and tries to grasp them by any means, and this thirst (or desire) in turn affirms and sustains the illusory existence of the subject as an entity separate from the integrated wholeness of the universe. The third truth teaches that suffering will cease if dualism is overcome and reintegration achieved, so that we no longer feel separate from the plenitude of the universe. Finally, the fourth truth explains that there is a Path that leads to the cessation of suffering, which is the one described by the rest of the Buddhist teachings.

All the various traditions are agreed that this basic problem of suffering exists, but they have different methods of dealing with it to bring the individual back to the experience of primordial unity. The Hinayana tradition of Buddhism follows the Path of Renunciation that was taught by the Buddha in his human form and later written down in what are known as the Sutras. Here the ego is regarded as a poisonous tree, and the method applied is like digging up the roots of the tree one by one. One has to overcome all the habits and tendencies that are considered negative and hindrances to liberation. There are thus, at this level, many rules of conduct, governed by vows that regulate all one's actions. The ideal is that of the monk or nun, who takes the

Sutra

Hinayana: the Path of Renunciation

maximum number of vows, but in any event, whether as a monk or a lay practitioner one's ordinary way of being is considered impure and to be renounced, in order, through the development of various states of meditation, to recreate oneself as a pure individual who has gone beyond the causes of suffering, an 'Arhat,' who returns no more to the round of births and deaths in conditioned existence.

From the point of view of the Mahayana, to seek only one's own salvation in this way, and to go beyond suffering whilst others continue to suffer, is less than ideal. In the Mahayana it is considered that one should work for a greater good, putting the wish for the realization of all others before one's own realization, **Mahayana**   and indeed continually returning to the round of suffering to help others get beyond it. One who practices in this way is called a Bodhisattva. Hinayana, or Lesser Vehicle, and Mahayana, or Greater Vehicle, are both parts of the Path of Renunciation, but their characteristic approaches are different. Since to cut through the roots of a tree one by one takes a long time, the Mahayana works more to cut the main root, so that the other roots may wither by themselves. The way to cut the main root is considered to be to discover the essential voidness both of the subject and of all objects, and to develop supreme compassion. It must be noted that, whereas the Mahayana posits the voidness of both the subject and its objects, and tells us to work toward realizing (or discovering) both, in the Hinayana only the voidness of the ego is posited and must be discovered.

In the Mahayana, the intention behind one's actions is considered as important as one's actions themselves, which is a different approach from that of governing all one's actions with vows as one does in the Hinayana. There is a story that illustrates this difference of approach very well. A wealthy merchant, who was a disciple of the Buddha, went with a very large caravan of other merchants and his servants to a certain island, to bring back for trade some of the gem stones for which this island was famous. On board ship, on the way back, the merchant learned that another passenger on the boat intended to kill all the hundreds of people on board, in order to be able to steal the cargo of jewels. The merchant knew the man, and knew that he was indeed capable of killing all those people, and he wondered what to do about it. In the end, despite the fact that he had taken a vow with the Buddha never to take the life of another being, he had no alternative but to kill the would-be robber. He was very ashamed of what he had done, and as soon as he returned home he went to the Buddha to confess his bad action. But the Buddha told him he had not done wrong, because his intention had not been to take life, but to save life. Furthermore, since he had in fact saved the lives of hundreds of people, and had saved the robber from the very negative karma of killing hundreds of people and the inevitable consequences of such a bad action, the Buddha explained that the merchant had in fact done a good action. Because the intention behind one's actions is considered of such importance in the Mahayana, all practice is undertaken for the benefit of others.

Zen Buddhism is a Mahayana path, and because it is often said to be a *non-gradual* method, people often think that it must be the same as Dzogchen, which is also sometimes spoken of as being a non-gradual path (although it is really more correct to say that it is neither gradual nor non-gradual); but the methods of the two teachings and the realizations obtained by them are fundamentally different.[1] Both the levels of the Path of Renunciation, Hinayana and Mahayana, can be said to work at the level of Body.

Tantra, on the other hand, works at the level of Energy, or 'Voice'. Energy is obviously less concrete than body, and less easy to perceive. It is harder to understand energy and how it functions than to understand the simple fact of suffering. A higher capacity is therefore needed to practice tantra. Although the term *tantra* and its Tibetan equivalent *gyü* has come to be used to denote the principal texts that contain tantric teachings, the true meaning of the word is 'continuity'[2], in the sense that although all phenomena are void, nevertheless phenomena continue to manifest. All tantric methods work with this continuation, taking the voidness of all phenomena, which the sutras work towards, as their basic assumption.

Tantra

From the sutra point of view, the relative dimension is an obstacle to be renounced in order to realize the absolute level of voidness. But tantra uses the relative to fuel progress on the path that leads beyond it, and its attitude to the passions renounced at the sutra level is expressed in the tantric saying, 'When there is more wood (passions) there is more fire (realization)'.

Vajrayana

The Outer Tantras

The Path of Purification

There are Outer and Inner tantras (also called Lower and Higher tantras in the schools other than the Nyingmapa, or Ancient School). Both these levels of tantra use visualization as a principal means, but the Outer tantras begin working at the level of the external conduct of the practitioner to bring about a purification of thought and action to prepare the practitioner to receive wisdom. The Outer tantras thus begin with what is called the Path of Purification, the first level of the Vajrayana, or 'Indestructible Vehicle'.

The Path of Transformation

The second level of the Vajrayana is the Path of Transformation, which begins with the third and last level of the Outer tantras and includes all the first two levels of the Inner tantras.

The Inner Tantras

These Inner tantras work once again on the basic assumption of the voidness of all phenomena, but the first two levels principally use inner yoga, working on the subtle energy system of the body, to bring about a transformation of the practitioner's whole dimension into the dimension of the realized being visualized in the practice. These methods were taught by the Buddha in a manifestation body, rather than by him in his physical body, as well as by other Sambhogakaya manifestations.[3]

Transmission of tantra is originally received through a manifestation of the Sambhogakaya dimension appearing to a master who has sufficient visionary clarity to perceive that dimension, and the method of practice used in tantra is also that of manifestation. Once one is initiated into the practice by the master, through visualization and the reintegration of one's subtle energy, one follows the example of the original transmission, and manifests oneself as the deity, entering the pure dimension of the mandala. Thus one realizes the Sambhogakaya oneself, transcending the mundane world of the gross elements, which are transformed into their essences. When one dies, one enters the dimension of light and color that is the essence of the elements, and in that purified state, though not active in the individual sense, one remains capable of continually benefiting other beings. It is said that the developed tantric practitioner is like a baby eagle which is ready to fly as soon as it hatches from the egg: as soon as one dies, at that very moment, without entering the Bardo, or intermediate state, one manifests as the divinity whose practice one has accomplished in one's lifetime. This realization is clearly different from the simple cessation of the round of birth and death which is aimed for in the Sutra practices.

To develop sufficient mastery of the inner energy and sufficient power of concentration to complete this process of transformation, however, requires long years of solitary retreat, and is very difficult to achieve in one's daily life, even though it is a quicker method than the methods of the Path of Renunciation, which take many lifetimes to complete.

But Dzogchen is neither sutra nor tantra. The basis for the communication of Dzogchen is introduction, not transformation into a manifestation as in tantra. And Dzogchen's principal practices work directly at the level of Mind in order to allow the individual to discover the primordial state to which he or she is introduced directly by the master, and to continue in it until the total realization of the Great Transfer or the Body of Light are achieved. It must be noted that, just as the realizations that are the Fruit of tantra are different from those that are obtained as a result of the applying the practices of the sutra vehicles, the Great Transfer and the Body of Light are particular to the Dzogchen teachings and do not correspond to the attainments of the practices of sutric and tantric vehicles. I shall not discuss these levels here, however, but in chapter eight on the Fruit of the Dzogchen teachings.

Dzogchen: The Path of Self-Liberation

Even though Dzogchen is a teaching that works principally at the level of Mind, practices of the Voice and Body are found in the Dzogchen teachings; but they are secondary to the practice of non-dual contemplation itself, and are used to bring the practitioner into this state. Only this contemplation can truly be called Dzogchen, but a Dzogchen practitioner may use practices from any of the levels of sutra or tantra, if they are found to be necessary to remove obstacles that block the state of contemplation.

The particular method of Dzogchen is called the Path of Self-Liberation, and to apply it nothing need be renounced, purified, or transformed. Whatever arises as one's karmic vision is used as the path. The great master Pha Tampa Sangye once said:

> It's not the circumstances which arise as one's karmic vision that condition a person into the dualistic state; it's a person's own attachment that enables what arises to condition him.

If this attachment is to be cut through in the most rapid and effective way, the capacity for self-liberation inherent in the primordial state must be brought into play. The term *self-liberation* should not, however, be taken as implying that there is some 'self' or 'ego' there to be liberated. It is a fundamental assumption, as we have already said, at the Dzogchen level, that all phenomenon are devoid of self-nature and it is understood that no phenomena has inherent existence. Self-Liberation, in the Dzogchen sense, means that whatever manifests in the field of the practitioner's experience is allowed to arise just as it is, without judgment of it as good or bad, beautiful or ugly. And in that same moment, if there is no clinging, or attachment, without effort, or even volition, whatever it is that arises, whether as a thought or as a conceptualization of a seemingly external event, automatically liberates itself, by itself, and of itself. Practicing in this way, the seeds of the poison tree of dualistic vision never even get a chance to sprout, much less to take root and grow.

So the practitioner lives his or her life in an ordinary way, without needing any rules other than one's own awareness, always remaining in the primordial state through integrating that state with whatever arises as part of experience—with absolutely nothing to be seen outwardly to show that one is practicing. This is what is meant by self-liberation, this is what is meant by the name Dzogchen—which means Great Perfection—and this is what is meant by non-dual contemplation, or simply contemplation.

Although in the course of my education in the monastic college in Tibet I came to study and practice all the various paths of Tibetan Buddhism, my master Changchub Dorje helped me to understand the particular value of the Dzogchen teachings, and so they are what I myself am principally concerned to teach.

The summary of the various paths of Sutra, Tantra, and Dzogchen presented in Appendix 1 has been included as an aid to getting clearly into view much of the terminology that is generally used in discussing the teachings. Despite the usefulness of such a presentation, however, there is a danger that some readers may make the false assumption that it implies a hierarchy of teachings with Dzogchen at the top. In fact, the whole layout could have been reversed, with Dzogchen at the bottom; or the chart, could be read from the bottom up, which is the sequence in which the gradual paths are presented and practiced, each stage having to be completed before the next can be approached. Dzogchen differs from the gradual paths because the master introduces the disciple directly to the Great Perfection, which is the heart of all the paths. But the reason why so many paths exist is that there is thus a teaching suited to the capacity of every individual. So, for example, for someone to whom the sutra teaching is best suited, that teaching can be said to be the 'highest', because that is the teaching that will work best for that individual. Any use of the words 'high', or 'highest', in relation to the Dzogchen teachings, should be read with this important proviso in mind.

It was the great eighth and ninth-century C.E. master Padmasambhava who was primarily responsible for enabling the Buddhist teachings to become established in Tibet, where obstacles had previously been created by the shamanic practitioners of the indigenous Bön traditions. Padmasambhava was a totally realized being who manifested an extraordinary birth in Ogyen, where he received visionary transmission of Dzogchen directly

Padmasambhava (Artist unknown.)

Guru Tragpo is a Heruka, and one of the principal wrathful forms in which Padmasambhava manifested to accomplish acts of power. (Line drawing by Nigel Wellings.)

from Garab Dorje as well as receiving the lineal or Kama transmission from the spiritual successors of Garab Dorje who were his contemporaries. Later, he travelled to India, where he absorbed and mastered all the tantric teachings being taught there at that time. He developed the capacity to transform himself into any form he chose, as well as all the other 'siddhis', or powers that may arise when the dualistic condition is overthrown. Thus, when he was invited to go to Tibet to further the spread of the Buddhist teachings there, he was able to overcome the obstacles that he encountered in the form of negative energies, by means of his own superior powers.

Bön shaman priests had the capacity to focus the various dominant energies of Tibet. They had used this power to make it difficult for the Buddhist teachings to take root there. Padmasambhava manifested in various forms to gain mastery of the local dominant energies himself, and to harness them to protect the Buddhist teachings, of which they then became the Guardians.

Since he was, however, beyond all limits, he did not consider it necessary to reject what was of value in the local traditions of Tibet, but instead created the conditions in which Buddhism could integrate with the local culture, with its sophisticated systems of cosmology, astrology, ritual and medicine, in the same way that Buddha Shakyamuni had taught within the framework of the Indian culture of his time, using it as the basis to communicate something essentially beyond culture. Thus, through Padmasambhava's influence and activity, there came into being that great confluence of spiritual traditions from Ogyen, India, and local Bönpo sources that is what we now know as the characteristically Tibetan form of Buddhism. The original disciples of Padmasambhava in Tibet did not consider themselves a school, or sect. They were simply practitioners of tantric Buddhism and Dzogchen. But when there arrived later different traditions of practice following other lines of transmission from Indian tantric masters, and these developed as schools, the original followers of Padmasambhava became known as the 'Nyingmapa', the 'Ancient Ones', or 'Ancient

The dakini Simhamukha is a wrathful form of the dakini Sangwa Yeshe or Guhyajnana. (Line drawing by Nigel Wellings.)

School'. One must be careful to avoid the mistake, however, of thinking that the Dzogchen teachings are a school or sect, in themselves, or that they belong to any school or sect. What is meant by *dzogchen* is always the primordial state, or a practice that enables us to discover and remain in that state. And although a lineage of transmission of this state from master to disciple does indeed exist, members of that lineage, all equally practitioners of Dzogchen, could be and still can be found in all the schools of Tibetan Buddhism, or among the practitioners of Bön, or belonging to no school or sect at all.

A few examples may help to make this clear. My master Changchub Dorje was without limits and independent of schools. As well as receiving transmission from his principal master Nyagla Padma Duddul, he received certain Dzogchen teachings and transmissions from a Bönpo Dzogchen master. In the Bön traditions there had existed a teaching of Dzogchen right from the dawn of Tibetan history, though this tradition was not as fully developed as that introduced by Garab Dorje. The Nyingmapa, or 'Ancient Ones', are the oldest of the four schools of Tibetan Buddhism, and absorbed the Dzogchen teachings at a very early date, still continuing to transmit them to the present day. So thoroughly has Dzogchen become identified with the Nyingmapa, however, that many have mistakenly assumed that Dzogchen belongs only to that school. Very many great exponents of Dzogchen have indeed manifested throughout the history of the Nyingmapa, such as in relatively recent times, Longchen Rabjampa (1303-1363) and Jigmed Lingpa (1729-1798), who were among the greatest scholars, historians, and spiritual teachers of Tibet. But another great Dzogchen practitioner was the head of the Karma Kagyüd school. This was Rangjung Dorje (1284-1339), the third Karmapa, who integrated the Mahamudra teachings transmitted in his school with the Atiyoga tradition of Dzogchen transmitted by the Nyingmapa, and the transmission of the teachings thus integrated continues to the present day in the Kagyüd school.

The Sakyapa school evolved in the same period as the Kagyüd, following other lines of transmission received from the

ༀ། །འདི་ག་ཉེ་དང་ལྡུག་གས་མ་ནཞི་སྐྱོ་དཔ་རུལ། ཕ་དང་ཕུ་བེམས་ཉེ་བ་བུ་ཕམ་དོ་ངས་གོ་ངས་ཏེ་
ཟོ་ལ། སྐྱི་ཐིག་གས་ཕྲ་བཀྲུ་ནཚོ་ཁས་ཟབ་བགུ་སྐྱོག། རང་བྱུ་ར་ཇེ་ཀྲ་ར་ཕྲུག་ལ་འཆས་པ། །

Tibetan wood-block print of the third Karmapa, Rangjung Dorje
(1284-1339), head of the Karma Kagyüd school, who integrated the
Mahayoga and Atiyoga traditions. (Artist unknown.)

Indian Mahasiddha tradition. The great tertön Jamyang Khyentse Wangpo and my own uncle Khyentse Chökyi Wangchug, who was an abbot of that school, were outstanding examples of the Dzogchen practitioners among the Sakyapa.

The most recently founded school, the Gelugpa, evolved as a reform movement which saw itself as returning from what were regarded as the excesses of tantrism to a reemphasis of the importance of the sutra teachings, and to the strict application of the Vinaya, or rules of monastic conduct laid down by the Buddha. It is often therefore assumed that Dzogchen must be very far from the Gelugpa ideal. Nevertheless, there have been many Dzogchen masters in that school, including Lobsang Gyatso, the great Fifth Dalai Lama (1617-82). He was the first Dalai Lama to hold the position of temporal ruler of Tibet as well as the spiritual role of his predecessors. It was he who began the building of the Potala Palace in its present form. He was a very great practitioner of Dzogchen. So it should, in general, be remembered that masters with principal allegiance to the one school, whilst fully maintaining that commitment, nevertheless freely received transmission from other traditions, and this in fact brought about a great cross-fertilization in Tibetan spiritual life and culture.

Tibetan wood-block print of the great Fifth Dalai Lama (1617-82), the first head of the Gelugpa school to be the temporal ruler of Tibet. He was a great Dzogchen practitioner. (Artist unknown.)

Chapter Five

With My Two Uncles Who Were Dzogchen Masters

First cut through the confusion of learning.
Then ponder the meaning of what was learned;
And lastly meditate its meaning as instructed.

—*Milarepa*

In Tibet masters could be found living in many different situations, but they had four principal types of life-styles: those who were monks, living in monasteries; those who lived a lay life, with their homes in villages; lay masters who lived as tent-dwelling nomads, travelling with their disciples, in some cases following their herds; and those who were yogis, often living in caves[1].

I personally received transmission not only from my principal master, but also from many others including my two uncles. My uncle Togden was a great yogi, a practitioner of Dzogchen. Like Changchub Dorje, he did not have an intellectual education involving study, and was not attached to any school. In Togden's case this was because his parents had decided when he was very young that he should be a silversmith, and so his whole education was aimed at preparing him for his work as a craftsman. But at a certain point he became seriously mentally disturbed, and none of the doctors could cure him. Finally, he was taken to see a Dzogchen master of that time, Adzam Drugpa [see plate 1], and as a result of contact with this master, he not only recovered from his illness but became a serious practitioner, a yogi who spent all his time in solitary retreats in isolated caves high in the mountains, where jaguars and leopards roamed.

I was sometimes allowed to stay with him as a child, and I remember that the leopards were particularly fond of butter, and that at night they would try to creep stealthily into the cave in which Togden stored his food to lick it up. I first learned Yantra Yoga in those high caves, as a very young boy, just copying Togden's movements. I first stayed with him when I was three years old, and I can remember my uncle practicing Yantra for hours stark naked, while I amused myself as children of that age will, occasionally playfully slapping or kicking my uncle's bare back, as part of my games, as he continued his practice unperturbed. When I was a little older, I learned the meaning of what he was doing.

The Practice of Chod

Togden wore his hair long and had a big bushy beard, so that when I later saw pictures Karl Marx I thought he bore a striking resemblance to my uncle, except that my uncle didn't wear glasses. He was an example of the kind of practitioner who becomes recognized as a master through the qualities he or she

Tibetan wood-block print of a practitioner of the Chöd, practicing in a charnel ground, sounding his damaru and thigh-bone trumpet. His vajra and bell are on the ground in front of him, together with an offering bowl made from a human skull. The dancing, grinning skeletons at the far right express a dynamic vision of death and change, viewed as an ecstatic dance of transformation, unchanging inner essence transcending the constant mutations of externals. Meditation on the impermanence of all phenomena should lead to a joyful freedom from attachment, and not to a morbid pessimism. (Artist unknown.)

manifests as a result of practice, rather than being recognized as the reincarnation of a previous master. When he was first sent to Adzam Drugpa he was so disturbed that he could hardly comprehend any of the teachings that were being given at the master's annual summer teaching retreat that was always held on the high plateau pasturelands. The teachings would take place surrounded by a village of tents, like a nomad encampment, that would arise for the duration of the retreat and then disappear again afterwards. By the time the retreat was over that summer, Togden had, with the help of Adzam Drugpa, been able to overcome his problem sufficiently to be ready to do some practice.

The master suggested that he make a solitary retreat, but because my uncle hadn't been able to follow the teachings, he didn't know what to do in such a retreat. This is how Adzam Drugpa resolved the difficulty: he sent my uncle to a cave about four days' journey away, telling him to stay there and practice until he sent for him, and he sent another disciple to show him the way to the cave. This other disciple had been following Adzam Drugpa for many years and was a serious practitioner. He was a simple man, not an intellectual, and he personally concentrated a great deal on the practice of the Chöd. This is a practice in which one works to overcome attachment and ego-clinging by making a mentally visualized offering of one's own physical body. The practice was developed by a great Tibetan lady practitioner, Machig Labdrön[2] (1055–1149), who came from a Bönpo family and who combined elements from the Bönpo traditions with teachings of the Prajnaparamita Sutra, of the tantras, and of the Dzogchen traditions that she received from her two root masters, Pha Tamba Sangye and Tragpa Ngönshe respectively, to produce a characteristically Tibetan form of practice which is a complete path in itself, but which is also practiced in conjunction with other methods.

Practitioners of Chöd are traditionally nomadic, travelling continually from place to place with a minimum of possessions, as mendicants, often carrying nothing more than the ritual instruments of a damaru, or two-sided drum, a bell, and a thigh-bone trumpet, and living in a small tent set up using a ritual

Machig Labdron (1055-1149) who first transmitted the Jod (Chod) as it is practiced today. She is holding a bell and damaru. (Line drawing by Nigel Wellings.)

trident (*katvanga*) as its tent pole, and four ritual daggers (purba) as its tent pegs. The practice is principally undertaken in lonely and desolate places, such as caves and mountain peaks, but particularly in graveyards and charnel grounds at night, when the terrifying energy of such places serves to intensify the sensation of the practitioner who, seated alone in the dark, summons all those to whom he owes a karmic debt to come and receive payment in the form of the offering of his body. Among the invited are Buddhas and illuminated beings, for whom the practitioner mentally transforms the offering into nectar, and all the beings of the six states of conditioned cyclic existence (samsara), for whom the offering is multiplied and transformed into whatever will be of most benefit and most pleasing, but also summoned are demons and evil spirits to whom the body itself is offered as a feast just as it is.

Internal 'demons' are all the usually latent fears, such as the fear of sickness or death, that can only be overcome when they are brought to the forefront of consciousness, but there also exist demons in the sense of negative energies that the practice enables the practitioner to magnetize and, ultimately, to master. We have an instinct for self-protection, trying to defend ourselves from imagined harm. But our attempt at self-protection ultimately causes us more suffering because it binds us into the narrow dualistic vision of self and other. By summoning up what is most dreaded and openly offering what we usually most want to protect, the Chöd works to cut us out of the double bind of the ego and attachment to the body. In fact the name *Chöd* means 'to cut'; but it is the attachment, not the body itself, that is the problem to be cut through. The human body is regarded as a precious vehicle for the attainment of realization.

The practitioner of Chöd who accompanied my uncle Togden to the cave in which he was to make his solitary retreat led him by an extremely circuitous route that travelled by way of so many lonely spots favorable to his practice that instead of the usual four days, it took them well over a month to reach their destination. And on the way, each day, in the course of their ordinary conversation, he communicated straightforward instructions on all aspects of practice, not just on the Chöd, to my uncle, so that when he was finally left alone, Togden knew exactly what he should do. My uncle stayed for several years in that retreat, and when he finally left it, he had already developed the remarkable powers that led people to give him the name, or title, of 'Togden', which means 'Accomplished Yogi', by which I always refer to him, although his given name was Ogyen Tendzin.

He continued thereafter to make frequent retreats, between which he travelled from place to place. His wanderings came to the attention of the Chinese authorities who were then making inroads into eastern Tibet, and they arrested him and called upon him to explain himself. Because of the way he was as an individual, my uncle was not able to give them an answer to their satisfaction, and so they decided he must be a spy. His execution was ordered, but despite several attempts to shoot him, it proved impossible to kill him. When he was released, the people of the area began to call him 'Togden'. He could also communicate so well with animals that even the wild and timid mountain deer that normally ran away from everyone freely came to him and stayed wherever he did. Less docile creatures also frequented his company. On one occasion when the King of Derghe himself came to visit Togden, his minister climbed up to Togden's cave to announce the arrival of the King and found an enormous mountain lion seated peacefully beside the yogi. The King had no choice but to share the company of that most royal of beasts if he wished to be received. This he did, with no little trepidation.

Living as he did, far from any centers of habitation, considerable hardship was involved for all those who gradually heard of Togden's reputation as a practitioner and came to seek him out to receive teachings from him. The same was also true of my other uncle, Khyentse Chökyi Wangchug, although the circumstances of his early life had been very different from Togden's. He had been recognized at an early age as a trulku, and was enthroned as the reincarnation of the abbot of four important monasteries. In this position he was expected to conform to a certain pattern of life involving administrative and even political duties, as well as fulfilling scholarly and ritual obligations. He, however, despite considerable opposition, preferred to spend his life in retreat, dedicating his life to practice. When in retreat he, too, lived in remote isolation, in his case in a cave above the snow line, where there was snow all the year round. But such was his reputation as a practitioner, and in particular as a tertön, or discoverer of texts and objects hidden in the past to be revealed later, that he was sought out by those determined to receive teachings from him.

Strange things frequently happened around Khyentse Chökyi Wangchug connected with his capacity as a tertön. On one occasion, when I was still quite young, I went to stay in a cave close to, but a little below, my uncle's. While there, I had a dream one night, in which a dakini appeared to me and gave me a small scroll of paper on which there was written a sacred text. She explained that the text was very important, and that on waking I should give it to my uncle. By this time my practice had already developed to the extent that I could maintain awareness throughout my sleep and dreams, and in this dream I knew that I was dreaming. I remember closing one of my fists around the scroll, and then closing the other fist tightly around the first.

The rest of the night passed uneventfully, and when I awoke at dawn, I found that my fists were still tightly clenched one around the other. When I opened my hands, I found that there really was a small scroll in the palm of one hand. I at once went in great excitement to knock on the door of my uncle's cave. It was not normally permitted to disturb him at such an early hour, as he would be engaged in his morning session of practice, but I was too excited to wait. He came to the door, and I explained what had happened and showed him the scroll. He looked at it for a moment, quite calmly, and said, 'Thank you. I was expecting this.' Then he went back to his practice as if nothing extraordinary had happened at all.

On another occasion, he asked my advice about a vision he had had of where a terma, a hidden text or object, would be discovered. He always very kindly showed great respect for my opinions, although I was still quite young. He was not sure whether to make a public announcement about the terma, or whether to go about finding it quietly. I felt it could be of benefit to many beings, in confirming and developing their faith, if many people knew about it and were present when it was found. My uncle agreed to this, and the announcement was made, declaring that the terma was located in a certain area, and that we would go to find it on a certain date. When the appointed day came, we went out, and were soon accompanied by a large crowd of people. The place my uncle had indicated was high up on the side of a mountain, and as he was an enormously fat man, he had to be carried by four men to get up there. Finally, he said that we had arrived close enough and pointed to a smooth, sloping rock face some way above us. He said that the terma was within the rock there. He then asked for a small ice-pick, of the sort that climbers use, and when one was given to him, he stood with it in his hand in silence for a few minutes, before throwing it with all his might up towards the rock face. The pick lodged firmly in what looked like solid rock, and held there. My uncle said that that was where the terma would be, and as everyone else watched, several of the younger men present made a ladder from a tree trunk, and set it in position to climb up. One young man then climbed carefully up and removed the pick. To everyone's amazement a certain amount of rock came away from what had looked like solid stone. My uncle then told the young man to search gently with the pick in the opening thus revealed. It was full of loose dry sand. My uncle told him to pull it out, and he very slowly did so. Then he stopped and gasped, perched high above us on the ladder. He said that he could see a smooth, round, luminous, white object. My uncle told him not to touch it. A blanket was then spread out below, held fairly taut between several people, and, using the pick, the young man up the ladder caused the object to fall into the blanket. My uncle then picked it up in a white silk scarf, and when he held it up we all saw the mysterious luminous white orb, made of no material known to us, and about the size of a large grapefruit.

When we returned home, my uncle closed the object in a special wooden container that was locked, and secured with a wax seal. He said that it would reveal itself further later. But when after several months, we opened the still sealed container, the object had mysteriously vanished. My uncle did not seem surprised, but said that the dakinis had taken it back, as the time was not yet ripe for its discovery and revelation.

As I have already said, strange things frequently happened around my uncle, and partly as a result of them many people sought teachings from him. It was a long climb to get to his cave from the forest far below, but nevertheless sometimes twenty or thirty people would make the tremendous effort to climb up to see him. Then his cave was very small, and all twenty or thirty people would have to squeeze inside, and sit really squashed together to hear him teach. Khyentse Chökyi Wangchug didn't plan to make it hard for people, it's just that these were the conditions he himself lived in. Then, at the end of the day, all those who had come for teachings would have to climb down the steep mountain-side in the dark—and we didn't have flashlights in Tibet. When they got to the bottom, they would spend the night in the forest, sleeping rough. There was no hotel there. And the next morning they would climb all the way up again to receive more teachings.

But even this hardship was nothing compared to the effort Milarepa had to make to receive teachings from his master Marpa[3] who made him build five towers and pull each one down again before he would give him any teaching. To understand why these people were prepared to endure all this hardship, we need to remember how fragile our lives are, and that death can come for any of us at any time. Knowing how we continue to suffer in life after life without understanding why we are suffering or how we can bring this suffering to an end, the enormous value of a master and his or her teaching becomes urgently clear.

It is not unusual for people to make great efforts and sacrifices to receive the teachings. But there is a tendency to want things made easy that is particularly common today. Here in this book it may seem that the explanations that follow of the Base, the

Path and the Fruit, as they are understood in the Dzogchen teachings, are complex, and that much effort is needed to understand them. Yet the effort required cannot be compared to the effort needed if one were to seek an explanation from a master such as Togden, Khyentse Chökyi Wangchug, or Marpa. No matter how clear a given explanation may be, without the active participation of the one who is to receive, nothing can be communicated. If an attempt is to be made sincerely to explain the nature of the universe and the nature of the individual, it cannot be expected that it will be as easy to read as a good story; and yet it need not be so very complicated either! There is a classic pattern of explanation of the teaching using a framework of interrelated concepts grouped in threes, and it is this pattern that the explanation given below will follow. The bones of this pattern can be shown simply in the form of a diagram:

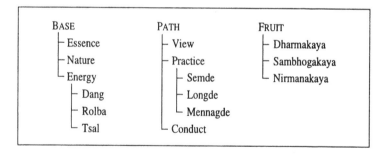

The Base, the Path, and the Fruit
=================================

The Base, the Path, and the Fruit

The Dzogchen teachings are also known in Tibetan by another name, *Thigle Chenpo*, or 'Great Thigle'. A *thigle* is a spherical drop-like form, with no dividing lines or angles, like the representation, below, of the circular mirror, or *melong*, made of five precious metals that is a particular symbol of the Dzogchen teachings and of the unity of the primordial state. So, although the teachings are divided into groups for the purpose of clear explanation, their fundamental unity, like the perfect sphere of the thigle, must not be forgotten. But within this fundamental

unity the groups of three are distinguished, each one intercon-
nected with all the others, as represented in the design shown
below right, with its triangular divisions, concentric circles, and
the *Gankyil*, or 'Wheel of Joy', whirling at the center. Around
the edge of this design, from the obverse of a contemporary
melong, the syllables *HA A HA SHA SA MA,* which close
the gates to the six realms, are written in an ancient script of
Zhangzhung.

Melong: front and obverse

Plate 1. Garab Dorje, the first Dzogchen master on this planet in this time cycle, and below him Adzam Drugpa, one of the great Tibetan Dzogchen masters of the late nineteenth and early twentieth centuries. (Thanka by Nigel Wellings; collection Bill Palmer; photo: Susan Bagley.)

Plate 2. Thanka showing the eighth-ninth century C.E. master Padmasambhava as a
Mahapandita, with his two principal female disciples Yeshe Tsogyal and Mandarava,
surrounded by scenes depicting masters involved in the early spread of the Buddhist
Dharma in Tibet. This thanka probably once belonged to a series thankas representing
the life of Padmasambhava. Enlarged details of this thanka, with explanation, appear
on the following pages. (Thanka by an unknown artist; collection John Shane; photo:
Susan Bagley.)

Plate 3. This detail from the thanka on the facing page shows Padmasambhava flanked by his two principal consorts. He holds a Dorje (Tibetan), or Vajra (Sanskrit), in his right hand, and a skull cup offering bowl in his left. Yeshe Tsogyal, on his right, holds the great master's ritual trident or Katvanga (Sanskrit). (Photo: Susan Bagley.)

Plate 4. This thanka detail shows Nubchen Sangye Yeshe who was a disciple of both Padmasambhava and Yeshe Tsogyal. He realized the practice of Yamantaka, one of the eight Herukas, or Desheg Kagyed, whose practices Padmasambhava transmitted to his principal disciples. Yamantaka is thus shown appearing above Nubchen Sangye Yeshe, just as in other details of the thanka the other Herukas are shown above the masters most associated with their practices. As a sign of his realization Nubchen Sangye Yeshe was able to pierce solid rock with his purba, or ritual dagger, shown in his left hand. (Photo: Susan Bagley.)

Plate 5. This detail from the thanka in plate 2 shows Yeshe Tsogyal, one of Padmasambhava's chief disciples and tantric consorts, giving two 'terma' or 'hidden treasures', one a reliquary, the other a text, to three dakinis who kneel respectfully before her. Two of the dakinis wear magic shawls of human skin. A being of the Naga class rises from his watery domain to receive treasures into his safe keeping (below right). Two terma can be seen already concealed in the rocks above Yeshe Tsogyal. (Photo: Susan Bagley.)

Plate 6. Detail of the thanka of the life of Padmasambhava showing his great Indian-born disciple and consort Mandarava, manifesting as a dancing dakini in a human body. (Photo: Susan Bagley.)

Plate 7. This thanka detail shows one of Padmasambhava's principal female disciples (probably Kalasiddhi) manifesting in a form similar to that of White Tara, to give teachings to disciples assembled before her. One disciple bears a pile of texts bound in silk. Above Kalasiddhi one of the eight Herukas, or Desheg Kagyed, manifests. (Photo: Susan Bagley.)

Plate 8. This thanka detail shows Vairochana (top left), the great translator contemporary of Padmasambhava, above whom appears the Heruka Tobden Nagpo in union with his consort. Below right, Yudra Nyingpo, Vairochana's principal disciple, is seated in meditation, surrounded by rays of rainbow light and luminous thigle, manifestations of his realized energy. Samantabhadra in union with his consort appears in the uppermost thigle, symbol of the Dharmakaya. To the left of Yudra Nyingpo is the figure of Pang Mipham Gönpo, a famous disciple of Yudra Nyingpo and Vairochana, who began to practice the Longde at the age of 85 and who many years later attained the Rainbow Body. (Photo: Susan Bagley.)

Plate 9. *Detail of thanka showing one of the foremost disciples of Vairochana, Palgi Yeshe, who was also the chief disciple of Jnanakumara, a translator colleague of Vairochana. Palgi Yeshe gained control of the Mamo class of Guardians, and is shown here with them appearing to him. Above him another of the eight Herukas manifests in union with his consort. (Photo: Susan Bagley.)*

Plate 10. *Detail of the thanka of the life of Padmasambhava and early spread of the Buddhist Dharma in Tibet, showing the great master holding a Vajra and offering a skull cup of nectar to a Heruka who manifests to him surrounded by flames. (Photo: Susan Bagley.)*

Plate 11. The great Fifth Dalai Lama (1617-82) is represented in this thanka. He was the first Dalai Lama to hold temporal power over all Tibet as well as spiritual authority as the head of the Gelugpa school. He was a great Dzogchen practitioner, outwardly manifesting conduct perfectly in accordance with his various responsibilities. He began the building of the great Potala palace, just outside Lhasa below and behind which, on an island at the centre of a lake, he began building a small secret temple for his personal use, called Zongdag Lukang, whose interior walls were covered with murals. (Thanka by unknown Tibetan artist; photo: Brian Beresford.)

Plates 12 and 13. Two details from the murals in the Fifth Dalai Lama's secret temple, Zongdag Lukang, showing yogis practicing Yantra Yoga. (Photos: Namkhai Norbu.)

Plates 14 and 15. These two details from the murals in the Fifth Dalai Lama's secret temple show yogis in various practice positions, with the Tibetan letter 'Ah', a symbol of the primordial state of mind, much used as an object of fixation, appearing in 'thigle' spheres of rainbow light. Different positions of the body, combined with specific breathing patterns, influence the flow of the individual's subtle energy, and thus the individual's state of mind. (Photo: Namkhai Norbu.)

Plate 16. This detail from the Thödgal mural in the Fifth Dalai Lama's secret temple shows yogis practicing in a mountain landscape, surrounded by various visionary apparitions manifesting as the function of their practice's progress. At the top left, the Buddha and five dakinis manifest in spheres of rainbow light, or 'thigle', below which a yogi is shown engaged in the practice of developing inner fire, or heat, as a means to realizing the union of sensation and voidness. Flames rise above his head from the central of his three principal channels, where a Tibetan letter 'Ah' manifests in a stream of five colored light. (Photo: Namkhai Norbu.)

Plate 17. This enlargement of the previous detail from the Thödgal mural shows more clearly, in two of the yogis' bodies, the position of the three principal channels of subtle energy just as they are visualized for the specific practice they are performing. The yogi who is seen from behind is practicing to integrate his energy with the element water. He is gazing at the moving water of a waterfall, while fixing his attention on the sound of the flowing water. The letter 'Ah' visualized at the centre of his body, superimposed over his central channel, is echoed by the external manifestation of a large watery letter 'Ah' to his right. (Photo: Namkhai Norbu.)

Plate 18. A Tibetan monk in India puts the finishing touches to a statue of the great Tibetan yogi poet Milarepa. Statues depicting Milarepa in this position are traditional, and are generally titled 'Milarepa listening to the sound of the Universe', as if his hand was raised to his ear to help him to hear. But it is more likely that he is actually using a yogic position in which his raised hand is pressing on one of the channels of subtle energy in his neck. (Photo: Brian Beresford.)

Plate 19. Detail of thanka showing Milarepa's principal lay disciple, Rechungpa (the 'lunar disciple'), kneeling to stare into a yak's horn lying on the ground within which Milarepa is sheltering from a hailstorm (see story, p. 156). (Photo: Brian Beresford.)

Plate 20. *His Holiness Tenzin Gyatso, the fourteenth Dalai Lama, at a Dzogchen teaching given by him in London in 1984, holding a crystal with a peacock feather attached above it. These were used as ritual implements in the initiation he gave, the crystal representing the practices of the Tregchöd, and the peacock feather representing Thödgal. (Photo: Brian Beresford.)*

Plate 21. *Detail from the Thödgal mural in the Fifth Dalai Lama's secret temple showing a yogi holding a crystal which reflects the sun's rays. Crystals are much used in the Dzogchen teachings as a symbol of the way in which the individual's own mind projects what appears to the individual lost in the illusion of samsara as a seemingly 'external' reality.*

Plate 22. Chögyal Namkhai Norbu practicing during a Spring 1984 retreat in the cave at Maratika in Nepal in which, many years before, Padmasambhava himself received transmission of and realized the practice of Amitayus, the Buddha of Long Life (see p. 123). (Photo: Carlo D'Angelo.)

Chapter Six

The Base

> It is quite impossible to find the Buddha anywhere
> other than in one's own mind.
>
> A person who is ignorant of this may seek
> externally, but how is it possible to find oneself
> through seeking anywhere other than in oneself!
>
> Someone who seeks their own nature externally is
> like a fool who, giving a performance in the middle
> of a crowd, forgets who he is and then seeks
> everywhere else to find himself.
>
> —*Padmasambhava (The Yoga of Knowing the Mind)*

Of the groups of three, the group known as 'The Base, the Path, and the Fruit'[1] is of central importance, and we shall now consider each of these in turn.

The Base: Essence, Nature, and Energy

The Base, or *Zhi* in Tibetan, is the term used to denote the fundamental ground of existence, both at the universal level and at the level of the individual, the two being essentially the same; to realize the one is to realize the other. If you realize yourself, you realize the nature of the universe. We have previously referred to the primordial state, experienced in non-dual contemplation, and it is in this state that the individual regains the experience of identity with the Base. It is called the Base because it is the base of all phenomena and because, being uncreated, ever pure and self-perfected, it is not something that has to be constructed. Although it is the uncreated and indestructible Base of the existence of each and every individual, it remains hidden to the experience of every being affected by the illusion of dualism: when this happens, it is temporarily obscured by the 'clouds' constituted by negative mental states in mutual interaction—for example, passions such as attachment and aversion—which arise from the basic ignorance of dualistic vision. However, the Base should not be objectified and considered as a self-existing entity; it is the insubstantial State or condition which serves as the basis of all entities and individuals, of which the ordinary individual is unaware but which is fully manifest in the realized individual.

In the teachings in general, not just in the Dzogchen teaching, it is considered that consciousness does not cease with the death of the physical body, but transmigrates, the karmic causes accumulated over countless lifetimes giving rise to further rebirths until the individual becomes realized, karma is transcended, and transmigration is brought to an end. The question of how and when this transmigration began is not so much spoken of, because it is considered more important to deal with those things that will actually be helpful in bringing the suffering of transmigration in conditioned existence to an end, rather than to waste one's precious time speculating about a first cause. At the time of the Buddha there was considerable debate amongst the Brahmin sects as to the precise nature of the Creator, and even as to whether a Creator existed. But instead of affirming or denying the existence of a Supreme Being as the first cause, the Buddha advised his disciples to leave aside all doubts and speculation and to strive to attain the state of Enlightenment in which questions disappear and clarity manifests.

At the level of what we ourselves actually experience in our lives it is clear where transmigration begins; it begins in any instant in which we enter into dualism just as it ends when we rediscover the primordial state, which is beyond all limits, including the limits of time, and of words and concepts. Nevertheless, the words of the *Song of the Vajra*[2] try to describe it:

The Song of the Vajra

Unborn, yet continuing without interruption,
neither coming nor going, omnipresent,
Supreme Dharma,
unchangeable space, without definition,
spontaneously self-liberating—
perfectly unobstructed state—
manifest from the very beginning,
self-created, without location,
with nothing negative to reject,
and nothing positive to accept,
infinite expanse, penetrating everywhere,
immense, and without limits, without ties,
with nothing even to dissolve
or to be liberated from,
manifest beyond space and time,
existing from the beginning,
immense ying[3], inner space,
radiant through clarity
like the sun and the moon,
self-perfected,
indestructible like a Vajra,
stable as a mountain,
pure as a lotus,
strong as a lion,
incomparable pleasure beyond all limits,
illumination, equanimity,
peak of the Dharma,
light of the universe,
perfect from the beginning.

The self-origination of the five elements and their essences

Just as the conditioned existence of the individual arises from karmic traces, so too does the existence of whole universes. The ancient Tibetan Bön tradition of cosmology, for example, explains that the space that existed before the creation of this universe was the latent karmic trace remaining from beings of previous universal cycles that had since gone into destruction. This space moved within itself, and the essence of the element wind was formed; the ferocious friction of this wind against itself gave rise to the essence of the element fire; resulting differences in temperature caused the condensation of the essence of the element water; and the swirling of these three already existing essences of elements gave rise to the essence of the element earth, in the same way that churning milk causes it to solidify into butter. This level of the essence of the elements is a pre-atomic level of existence as light and color. From the interaction of all the essences of the elements, the actual elements at an atomic, or material, level are formed, in the same manner and sequence that the essences of the elements were formed. Then from the interaction of the material, or atomic, elements, what is called the 'Cosmic Egg', made up of all the various realms of being, is formed. These realms are the traditional six dimensions of conditioned existence: those of the Gods and Demi-Gods (including the higher Divinities and Nagas), Humans, Animals, Frustrated Spirits, and the Hell Beings.

If the essences of all the elements (and thus the elements themselves[4] and all the various realms) arise from space, which is the latent karmic traces of past beings, this space is clearly not beyond karma and the conditioned level of existence, and in that case what is said about the Base couldn't be said about it. You couldn't say that it has been fundamentally pure and self-perfected from the very beginning.

So the Base can be compared to space in so far as it is that which allows for the manifestation of entities, but it cannot be identified with conditioned space. What we could say is that the Base is that which allows conditioned space to manifest, and it could thus be compared to the essence of the element space, which we could say is '...unborn, yet continuing without interruption, neither coming nor going, omnipresent, beyond space and time, existing from the beginning...' in the words of the *Song of the Vajra*.

The Dzogchen teachings themselves view the process of cosmic origination in a way that is parallel to, but slightly different from, the Bön tradition. In the Dzogchen teachings, it is considered that the primordial state, which is beyond time, and beyond creation and destruction, is the fundamentally pure base of all existence, both at the universal and the individual levels. It is the inherent nature of the primordial state to manifest as light, which in turn manifests as the five colors, the essences of the elements. The essences of the elements interact (as explained in the Bön cosmology) to produce the elements themselves, which make up both the individual's body and the whole material dimension. The universe is thus understood as the spontaneously arising play of the energy of the primordial state, and may be enjoyed as such by an individual who remains integrated with his or her essential inherent condition, in the self-liberating, self-perfected state, the state of Dzogchen.

But if, through fundamental misperception of reality, the individual enters into the confusion of dualism, primordial consciousness, which is in fact the source of all manifestation (even of dualistic consciousness and, in fact, of all phenomena), itself becomes obscured. The individual's deluded mind then mistakes the manifestations of its own pure, innate primordial awareness for an external reality existing separately from itself, which it endlessly, and ultimately unsuccessfully, attempts to manipulate, trying in vain to bring an end to the continual underlying sense of dissatisfaction and unease which is the inevitable experience of the obscuration of pure awareness. The experience of underlying dissatisfaction (or 'dukha', in Sanskrit) that unavoidably arises with a deluded mind, continues, no matter how 'successful' the individual becomes in dealing with his or her world in materialistic terms, until the individual regains the experience of the primordial state.

All the various passions arise from the fundamental misperception of reality just described, and the passions once they have arisen continually condition the individual into dualism, deepening the individual's sense of confusion about the nature of reality. This is why samsara, the endless round of conditioned existence, is often described in the teachings as being a 'vicious cycle'.

The Dzogchen teachings, in the explanations of the Base, the Path, and the Fruit, set out to show how the illusion of dualism has come about, how it can be undone, and what the experience of an individual is when it is undone. But all examples used to explain the nature of reality can only ever be partially successful in describing it because it is, in itself, beyond words and concepts. As Milarepa said, we may say that the essential nature of the mind is like space, because both are empty, but mind is aware, while space is not. Realization is not knowledge about the universe, but the living experience of the nature of the universe. Until we have such living experience, we remain dependent on examples, and subject to their limits.

We could say that the Base is like a mysterious object that I am trying to describe to you. I might say that the object is white and 'sort of round', and then you'll get a certain idea of it. But then, the next day you might hear another description given by someone else who has seen the object, and then you'll change your mind according to their description, thinking perhaps that it's rather more oval than round, and the color of mother of pearl rather than white. Fifty descriptions later, you're not really any the wiser about the object, still changing your mind each time you hear it described. But if you once see the object for yourself, then you know for sure what it is like, and you understand that all the descriptions were right, in part, but none really could catch the whole nature of that mysterious object. Something similar happens with the descriptions of the Base, or primordial state, which is, and never ceases to be, the true inherent condition of the individual, pure from the beginning, and remaining so, even while the superficial consciousness of a deluded being is immersed in dualism and enmeshed in the passions.

Now that we have considered the meaning of the term *Base* as it is understood in the Dzogchen teachings, we can begin to consider how this Base manifests as the individual and the universe he or she experiences. All levels of the teachings regard the individual as being made up of Body, Voice, and Mind. The perfected states of these which manifest in realized individuals are symbolized by the Tibetan syllables *Om, Ah* and *Hum*, respectively. Body includes the whole material dimension of the individual, while Voice is the vital energy of the body, known as *prana* in Sanskrit, and *lung* in Tibetan, the circulation of which is linked to the breathing. Mind includes both the mind that reasons, and the nature of the mind, which is not subject to the limits of the intellect. The body, voice, and mind of an ordinary being have become so conditioned that he or she has become completely caught up in dualism. Such a being's

Pure and impure vision dualistic perception of reality is called impure or karmic vision, as it is conditioned by the karmic causes continually manifesting as a result of one's past actions, to the extent that one lives enclosed in the world of one's limits, like a bird in a cage. But a realized individual, who has discovered the true condition of the Base which was formerly obscured, and who lives in and for this condition, is said to have 'pure vision'.

The self-perfect clarity of the pure vision of the primordial state in realized individuals has allowed them to not limit themselves to only giving a Direct Introduction to the state in which the true condition of the Base is fully manifest, but has permitted them to also give a Symbolic Introduction to the Base, as well as an Oral Introduction in which it is explained verbally.

The oral explanation describes the functioning of the Base in terms of three aspects or 'Three Wisdoms': the Essence, Nature and Energy. And in order to symbolize the functional

Om, Ah, Hum (Calligraphy by Namkhai Norbu.)

Tibetan woodblock print showing Yama, the god of death, holding the 'Wheel of Existence.' At the center, the cock, snake, and pig symbolize the 'Three Poisons': dualistic mind, or ignorance (pig), which gives rise to aversion (snake) and attachment (cock), which lock an individual into a vicious cycle of self-sustaining suffering (Sanskrit: samsara). In the next circle, proceding outwards from the center, beings are shown either progressing upwards towards realization through spiritual practice, or falling downward, becoming more caught up in transmigration in the six realms of conditioned existence, which are shown in the next and widest circle. The three higher realms are shown in this version of the Wheel in two segments of the circle to the left and

aspect of the Base that each of these Three Wisdoms represents, a mirror is traditionally used: the voidness which allows the mirror to 'fill itself' with any content illustrates the Essence; the mirror's capacity to reflect represents the Nature, and the particular appearances that are reflected in the mirror symbolize the Energy.

Essence

The aspect of the Base that is referred to as the 'Essence' is its fundamental voidness. Practically speaking, this means that, for example, if one looks into one's own mind, any thought that arises can be seen to be void in the three times, past, present, and future. That is to say, if one looks for a place from which the thought came, one finds nothing; if one looks for a place where the thought stays, one finds nothing; and if one looks for a place where the thought goes, one finds nothing—voidness. It is not that there is some void that could be said to be some sort of *thing*, or *place* itself, but rather that all phenomena, whether mental events or apparently *external* actual objects, no matter how solid they may seem, are in fact essentially void, impermanent, only temporarily existing, and all 'things' can be seen to be made up of other things, in turn made up of other things, and so on. From the enormously large, to the infinitely small, and everywhere in between, everything that can be seen to exist can be seen to be void.

And by way of an example, this voidness is said to be like the fundamental purity and clarity of a mirror. A master may show the disciple a mirror and explain how the mirror itself does not judge the reflections arising in it to be either beautiful or ugly: the mirror is not changed by whatever kind of reflection

---

right of the 12 o'clock position. The gods' and demigods' realms are shown as one on the left, and the human realm is shown on the right. Continuing clockwise, there are the realm of the pretas, or continually frustrated spirits, the realm of hell beings, and the realm of the animals. The human realm is the most favorable for progress to realization. The outer circle symbolizes the twelve links of the 'Chain of Interdependent Origination', which explains how in every instant dualistic experience is solidified out of the open space of primal awareness through fundamental misperception of reality and the ensuing mental processes, thus creating the illusion of conditioned existence in the six realms. (Artist unknown.)

may arise, nor is its capacity to reflect impaired. It is then explained that the void nature of the mind is like the nature of the mirror, pure, clear, and limpid, and that no matter what arises, the void essence of the mind can never be lost, damaged, or tarnished.

Although voidness in the sense explained above is the essential underlying condition of all phenomena, phenomena—whether mental events or 'real' objects experienced as something external—continue to manifest. Just as reflections, even though they are empty, keep appearing in a mirror, things continue to exist and thoughts keep arising. This continuous arising is the aspect of the Base that is called 'Nature'. The Nature of the Base is to manifest, and in order to illustrate this nature it is compared to the capacity of a mirror to reflect all that is put in front of it.

The master may use a physical mirror in order to show that, no matter whether what is reflected is good or bad, beautiful or ugly, the capacity to reflect inherent to the mirror functions as soon as an object is put in front of it. Then he will explain that the same happens with what is termed 'nature of mind', which is discovered in non-dual contemplation. Any thought or event may arise, but the nature of mind will not be conditioned by it and will not enter into judgment: it will simply reflect what arises, just as a mirror does, according to its own nature.

Nature

So the Zhi, the Base, the fundamental condition of the individual and of existence, is in essence void, and yet its Nature is nevertheless to manifest. How it manifests is as Energy, and by way of example, this Energy is compared to the reflections that arise in a mirror. The master may once again show a mirror to the disciple and explain how the reflections that arise in it are the energy of the mirror's own inherent nature manifesting visibly.

Energy

Now, although in order to explain the Base we may artificially separate its Essence, Nature, and Energy, the example of the mirror shows that these three aspects are interdependent and cannot be separated from each other. In fact, a mirror's primordially pure voidness, its clear capacity to reflect and the reflections that arise in it are inseparable and are all essential to the existence of what is known as a 'mirror'.

If it were not empty, the mirror would not reflect; if it did not have a clear capacity to reflect, how could it manifest reflections? And if it could not manifest reflections, how could we say it was a mirror? The same is true of the three aspects of the Base: Essence, Nature, and Energy are inseparable.

How the Energy manifests: Dang, Rolba, Tsal

Energy manifests in three characteristic ways, which are known as Dang, Rolpa, and Tsal. These terms are untranslatable, and we have to use the Tibetan words. They are explained with three examples: the mirror, the crystal ball, and the crystal-prism.

Dang

A mirror has neither form nor color. Yet when a red cloth is placed in front of it, the mirror seems red, and with a green cloth in front of it, it seems green, and so on. Thus, although a mirror's voidness is essentially infinite and formless, the mirror may fill itself with any content. The same happens with the individual's energy: although at the Dang level it is essentially infinite and formless, it is clear that it has the capacity to adopt any form.

In fact, although essentially our energy is totally formless and free from any duality, the karmic traces contained in our stream of consciousness give rise to the forms that we experience as body, voice, and mind, as well as to those that we perceive as an external environment—whose characteristics are in both cases determined by the causes accumulated during numberless lives. The problem is that these karmic traces also give rise to the dualistic delusion and the attachment that cause us to be utterly unaware of our own true condition, so that we experience a radical separation between our person—body, speech, and mind—and that which we take for an external world. This causes us to experience both ourselves and the 'world around us' as absolute, self-existing realities. The result of this delusion is what is known as 'karmic vision'.

When freed from this illusion, the individual experiences his or her own nature as it is and as it has been from the very beginning: as an awareness free from any restrictions and as an energy free from any limits or form. To discover this is to discover the *Dharmakaya* or 'Body of Truth', which is better rendered as 'Body of the True Nature of Reality'.

This type of manifestation of the individual's energy is illustrated with the example of a crystal ball. When an object is placed near a crystal ball, an image of the object may be seen inside the ball, so that the object itself seems to be found inside it. The same may happen with the energy of the individual, which has the potentiality to appear as an image experienced 'internally', as though it were seen 'with the eye of the mind', although what appears is truly neither 'inside' nor 'outside': no matter how vivid this seemingly 'internal' image may be, it is, just as in the previous case, a manifestation of the individual's own energy, this time in the form of *Rolpa* energy.

Rolpa

It is on the basis of the functioning of this type of manifestation of energy that many of the practices of Thödgal and of the Yangthig work. (These practices will be discussed in following chapters.) It is the source of the one hundred peaceful and wrathful deities which, according to the *Bardo Thödrol* or *Tibetan Book of the Dead*[6], arise in the experience of the *chönyid* bardo (or bardo of the *Dharmata*); and it is also the original source of the deities that are visualized by practitioners of the Path of Transformation in order to transform their impure vision into pure vision.

Finally, it is precisely this level of their own energy that realized individuals experience as the Sambhogakaya or 'Body of Wealth'[7]. The wealth referred to is the fantastic multiplicity of forms that may manifest at this level, corresponding to the essence of the elements, which is light and which realized individuals do not perceive in dualistic terms.

Tsal is the manifestation of the energy of the individual him or herself, as an apparently 'external' world. But, in fact,

Tsal

the apparently external world is a manifestation of our own energy, at the level of Tsal. Together with the arising of dualism, however, there simultaneously arises the illusion of a self-existing individual who feels separate from a world which he or she experiences as external. The fragmented dualistic consciousness takes the projections of the senses for objects existing independently and separately from the illusory 'self' with which it identifies and to which it clings.

The example used to illustrate the illusory nature of our sense of separateness establishes a parallel between the way in which the individual's energy manifests and what happens when a crystal-prism is placed in the light of the sun: when the sun's light falls on a crystal, it is reflected, refracted and decomposed by it, causing the appearance of rays and forms in the colors of the spectrum which seem to be separate from the crystal, but which are actually functions of the crystal's own nature.

In the same way, what appears as a world of apparently external phenomena is the energy of the individual him or herself, as perceived by his or her senses. In truth, there is nothing external to, or separate from, the individual, and all that manifests in the individual's field of experience is a continuum, fundamentally free from duality and multiplicity: this is precisely the 'Great Perfection' that is discovered in Dzogchen.

For a realized individual, the level of manifestation of energy called 'Tsal' is the dimension of the *Nirmanakaya* , or 'Body of Manifestation'. But we must keep in mind that neither the Dang, Rolpa, and Tsal forms of the manifestation of energy, nor the Dharmakaya, the Sambhogakaya, and the Nirmanakaya, are separate from each other. Limitless, formless Dang energy, the correct understanding of which is the Dharmakaya, manifests on the level of the essence of the elements, which is light, as the nonmaterial forms of the Rolpa energy, the correct understanding of which is the Sambhogakaya, which can only be perceived by those having visionary clarity. On the 'material' level, it manifests as the forms of Tsal energy, which deluded individuals perceive as external to their consciousness, as solid and material, but the correct understanding of which is the Nirmanakaya. (The 'correct understanding' referred to in each case is clearly not intended to mean a mere intellectual understanding, but refers to a shift from deluded consciousness to the non-dual experience of reality as it is.)

So, to say that the Enlightened ones possess three *kaya* or bodies does not mean they have three physical bodies in different dimensions, or three levels, like a statue; the *kaya* are the three modes of the manifestation of the energy of every individual, as experienced in realization. These three *kaya* will be considered later on in further detail.

The examples just given above are among the ways in which the master may give the disciple a 'Symbolic Introduction' to the Base; and the explanations of the three aspects of the Base, and the way in which the Base manifests as the three types of energy, are how he or she gives the disciple the 'Oral Introduction' to it.

This is the open secret, that everyone can discover for themselves: we live our lives, as it were, inside out, conceiving ourselves as an 'I' that we take to be absolutely separate from a world that we regard as external, and trying to manipulate that world in order to achieve satisfaction. But as long as we remain in the dualistic state, our experience will continue to be characterized by an underlying sense of lack, fear, anxiety, and dissatisfaction.

When, on the other hand, one goes beyond the dualistic level, anything is possible. Near the cave of Milarepa there lived a very scholarly Tibetan monk who saw himself as being very intelligent. He believed he could overcome everything with his intellect, but the strange thing was that everyone went to receive teachings from Milarepa who had never studied anything, and no one came to see this monk. The monk was very jealous, and went to see Milarepa to debate with him. He wanted to expose him with a few well-chosen words of argument, so he asked: 'Is space material or immaterial?' Milarepa replied: 'It's material'. The monk thought to himself: 'Now I've shown him up as a complete idiot!' and was preparing to debate some more in the same way, when Milarepa picked up a stick and began banging on empty space as if it were a drum. The monk then asked: 'Is a rock material or immaterial?' Milarepa replied by passing his hand through a rock. The amazed monk became his disciple.

The intellect is a valuable tool, but it doesn't extend to the whole of our reality. In fact it can be a trap preventing our gaining access to the most profound aspects of our own nature. When I was young, I met a very strange master whose activities were as unfathomable to the intellect as Milarepa's, though his life story was very different. He had formerly been a monk in a Sakyapa monastery, which like all monasteries had certain very strict rules. This monk had broken the rules in a very serious way by having a relationship with a woman, and he had been expelled from the monastery. He felt bad about what had happened, and so he went very far away, but on his travels he met some masters, received some teachings from them, and became a serious practitioner. Then he returned to his native village, but the monastery there wouldn't take him back in, so his relatives built him a little retreat hut on the mountain side. He lived there practicing quietly for several years, and became known to everyone as 'The Practitioner'.

But after a few more quiet years he suddenly seemed to go crazy. One day while he was doing his practice, he began to throw all of his books out of the window; then he burned them, smashed up all his statutes, turned everything upside down, and partly destroyed his retreat house. People began to call him 'The Lunatic'. Then he disappeared, and no one saw him for three years. At the end of that time, somebody came across him quite by chance. He was living in a very remote spot, right at the top of the mountain. Everybody wondered how he had managed to survive and get enough to eat up there all that time, because nothing grew there and normally nobody ever went there. So people began to take an interest in him and to visit him. Although he refused to communicate with them, the way that he lived convinced people that he wasn't crazy. Instead of calling him 'The Lunatic', they began to speak of him as a realized being, a saint.

My uncle the Sakyapa abbot, Khyentse Chökyi Wangchug, heard about him, and decided to visit him, taking me and a few other people with him. It took us fifteen days on horseback to get to the village below the mountain where the strange master lived. From there we would have to climb up on foot as there was no track to the mountain top, which was very difficult to reach. The people of the area told us that some days previously, a very famous Kagyüd trulku incarnation had gone up there to visit, but when he arrived, instead of receiving teaching, he'd been driven off with a barrage of stones and some of the monks in his party had been quite badly hurt. They also told us that this master up there had dogs, and that some of them were fierce and would bite. All of the local people were afraid of going to see him, and by the time we'd heard all this, quite frankly, so were we.

My uncle was a very fat man, and to climb the steep mountain side without a path took us a very long time. We were always slipping and sliding back down on the loose rock. When we had almost reached the top, we could hear the master talking somewhere, but we couldn't see a house anywhere. Then, when we finally arrived at the very peak of the mountain, we saw a kind of rudimentary stone structure. You couldn't really call it a house, it was more like a big dog kennel roofed over with stones, with big open holes in three of its sides. It wasn't high enough for anyone to be able to stand up in. We could hear the master still talking inside, but we couldn't imagine who he might be talking to.

Then he turned and saw us approaching, so he at once pretended to be asleep, pulling a blanket up over his head. He really did seem crazy, but we cautiously went even closer. When we got quite close we waited a few minutes and then he suddenly pulled the blanket away from his face and looked at us. His enormous staring eyes were bloodshot, and his hair stood wildly on end. I found him really terrifying. He began to speak, but we couldn't understand what he was saying, even though he was a Tibetan like us. It was not that he was speaking in a local dialect that we didn't understand; we knew the dialect of that area quite well. He spoke for about five minutes without interruption, but I only understood two phrases. Once he seemed to be saying 'in the middle of the mountains,' but then what he said next was incomprehensible again. The next phrase I caught seemed to be 'valley' and then nothing meant anything again. I asked my uncle what he had understood, but he had only caught the same two fragments, and none of the other people with us had understood any more either.

My uncle crawled in through the largest of the openings in the stone wall, perhaps with the intention of asking for a blessing, to see what the reaction would be. The hut was very small and he was very big, and the strange master stared right into his face. My uncle had brought some sweets with him, and he offered two of these to the master, who took just one. The master had a kind of earthenware pot by his side. He put the sweet in the pot and offered it back to my uncle. My uncle just stayed in there waiting. Then the master pulled out from a fold in his tattered clothes a piece of old woolen cloth which he had clearly used for blowing his nose, and he presented this to my uncle. My uncle accepted it respectfully and continued waiting, until the master gave him a very fierce look, at which my uncle decided it was wisest to come out.

It was then my turn to go in. I was very frightened, but in I went, with a packet of biscuits which my uncle had given me to offer. I offered the packet, but the master wouldn't take it. I thought: 'Maybe I should have opened the packet first,' so I opened it and offered him some biscuits. He took one and put it in his pot. I managed to get a look into the pot, and saw that it was full of water, but that it also contained a bit of everything, some tobacco, some peppers, and my uncle's sweet, together with my biscuit. I don't know if he ate from this pot or if he just kept things in it, but there was nothing in that hut that suggested the normal domestic activities of preparing and cooking food, even if its inhabitant could have found some up there. I stayed a little longer taking all this in, until with a ferocious look the master gave me a sort of half broken earthenware teapot which he used as a piss-pot, and then, taking this gift with me, I left to rejoin my uncle and the others outside. We'd been there about twenty minutes in all, and we stood outside looking in at him.

Then he began speaking to us again incomprehensibly and pointing, and we got the idea that he was trying to tell us to go in that direction. We waited there a little longer, when he suddenly said, rather angrily and quite coherently, 'Better to go!' My uncle turned to me and the rest of our little group and said: 'Maybe we had better do as he says', and we all set off in the direction in which the strange master had pointed. It wasn't the way we had come and would have to go back, and we hadn't the faintest idea where we were going or why, but my uncle said that there might be something behind what the master had said.

It was very rough going but we clambered along and down from that peak for several hours, to the place where the mountain began to rise again towards the next peak. In what you might call the saddle between the two peaks there was a heavily forested area, and just before we got down to that we heard what sounded like someone groaning and crying out. We hurried forward and found a hunter who had fallen from the rocks and broken his foot. He was unable to walk, and so some of our group carried him back to where his family lived, which was some considerable distance away. My uncle suggested that the rest of us go back to see the strange master. 'Perhaps he'll give us some teaching now,' he said. But when we got back to the strange master's hut, far from saying anything like, 'Well done!', he just told us to go away.

But the fact that a master like this was not committed to teaching human beings doesn't necessarily mean that he wasn't teaching at all. He might have been living in that strange way while manifesting in another dimension to teach beings other than humans. In that way he could have been giving teaching to more beings than there are in a whole huge city, while we did not have the capacity to perceive such activity. Garab Dorje, for example, taught the Dzogchen teachings to the dakinis before teaching them to human beings. In the bardo, the intermediate state after the death of the physical body and before the next rebirth, beings possess only a mental body to which no organism whatsoever corresponds on the solid, material plane. It is possible that this master who seemed so strange to us was teaching such beings. When we understand the non-dual nature of reality as described in the explanations of the Base as Essence, Nature, and Energy, and know how the Energy of the individual manifests as Dang, Rolpa and Tsal, we can understand how someone who has reintegrated their Energy is capable of actions not possible for an ordinary being. Then the actions of such a master no longer seem so incomprehensible.

Chapter Seven

The Path

Some people spend
the whole of their life
preparing to practice.

Then the end of their life comes,
and they are still preparing.

So they begin their next life
without ever having completed
all these preparations!

—*Tragpa Gyaltsen, a great master of the Sakyapa school*

The second aspect of the principal group of three—the Base, the Path, and the Fruit—is the Path. Everything in the Path is concerned with how one can work to bring oneself out of the dualistic condition, to realization. Because even if the master has transmitted an Introduction to the primordial state directly, and has given an explanation of the state and how it manifests, the problem is that we ourselves remain closed up in the cage of our limits. We need a key, a way to open the cage, a method with which to work in order to become established in that which the Introduction had allowed us to glimpse. This key is the Path, or *Lam* in Tibetan, which itself can be seen to have three aspects.

Tawa: the 'View', or 'Vision' of the true condition of the individual and of all phenomena

The first aspect of the Path is the Tawa: the 'View', or 'Vision' of the true condition of the individual and of all phenomena.

The reason the Tawa is sometimes referred to as the 'Vision' of the true condition, rather than as the 'View', is because in Dzogchen the term Tawa does not refer to a philosophical or intellectual point of view. When people speak of a 'view' they often mean a philosophical position held by a person or school. The Madhyamika philosophy, for example, is often spoken of as being the 'viewpoint, or view, of Nagarjuna'. But in Dzogchen, rather than the View meaning that we just study, absorb and subscribe to a theoretical philosophical viewpoint, what is necessary is that we observe ourselves so that we can really discover for ourselves what our true condition is.

The direct, non-dual, non-conceptual knowledge of this true condition—our absolute nature, fundamentally pure from the beginning, and completely free from all conditioning, never lost or stained even though it is veiled in the dualistic experience of samsara—is true Tawa or Vision of Dzogchen; and when this Vision becomes stable for us, we overcome the limitations that create and sustain the cage of our limited sense of self, or ego.

But if we are caught up in dualism, the first thing we need to do is to discover exactly how we are so thoroughly conditioned, and how our limitations confine us in the cage of dualism. So the Tawa of Dzogchen also implies, at the relative level, that we observe ourselves thoroughly at the levels of our body, voice, and mind, and confront all our problems, and this may be neither easy nor pleasant.

There are many practical problems relating to our work, our living conditions, getting enough to eat, our health, and so on. These could be called the problems of the body. Then there are the problems of the voice, or energy: nervousness, neuroses, psychosomatic problems, and various other types of disturbances.

And even if we are physically fit and materially well-off, there are still the problems of the mind. These mental problems are so many and can be so subtle and hard to see—there are all kinds of games that we play in order to maintain, impose and boost our egos.

We play these games imagining that through them we will somehow improve our situation, but in fact all we succeed in accomplishing is building a cage and locking ourselves inside it. And once we are in the cage the problem then becomes that we deceive ourselves into no longer even being able to see that it is there. So the first step towards getting out of this self-created cage is that we must become aware that it is there, and this can only be done by observing ourselves all the time. This is another reason why the mirror or *melong* is such an important symbol in Dzogchen. Besides representing the true condition of the Base and the inseparability of the two truths—relative and absolute[1]—the mirror also serves as a reminder to observe one's own condition at all times.

There is a Tibetan proverb which runs like this:

> On someone else's nose
> one won't fail to notice
> the presence of even
> something as small as an ant.
> But on one's own nose
> one won't even see
> something as big as a yak.

That may indeed be the way in which we human beings often tend to behave, but it's not the right outlook according to the Tawa of Dzogchen. According to the Tawa of Dzogchen one should not look outwards and criticize others; one should observe oneself, and by observing oneself, one becomes aware of one's cage.

But it's not enough just to know that the cage is there; one must sincerely want to break out of it, and then actually begin working to that end.

The way to break out of the cage, according to the Dzogchen teachings, is to establish the Tawa or Vision of the true condition of the individual and of all phenomena—which dissolves all illusory limits—and this process can be explained in terms of Garab Dorje's Three Principles: access to the Tawa is gained through receiving the Direct Introduction to the primordial state, or Base, from the master; and it is through repeatedly returning to the Tawa that the practitioner is enabled to 'not remain in doubt' about the true nature of all experiences; and then he or she endeavors to dwell uninterruptedly in the Vision or Tawa itself, which means 'continuing' in the primordial state.

But whenever one does not find oneself in the primordial state one should constantly observe oneself without distraction, governing one's behavior with the kind of 'relative' self-observing awareness that recognizes the consequences of one's actions, and one should maintain this awareness for as long as the 'absolute' spontaneous non-dual awareness of the primordial state, that is one's true condition, is not present.

Although we have just considered the Tawa in terms of all three of Garab Dorje's Principles, it might be more usual to regard the first two Principles as referring to the Tawa, while the third Principle refers more specifically to the Gompa and the Chöpa, which will be explained in the next two sections of this book. As we shall see, the Gompa could be defined as 'remaining in the Tawa', while the Chöpa could be defined as 'behavior arising from the Gompa'.

Gompa: practice

> The great Dzogchen master Yungtön Dorje Pal was asked: 'What meditation do you do?' And he replied: 'What would I meditate on?'
>
> So his questioner concluded: 'In Dzogchen you don't meditate, then?'
>
> But Yuntön Dorje Pal replied: 'When am I ever distracted [from contemplation]?'

The distinction between what is meant by the terms *meditation* and *contemplation* is an essential one in Dzogchen. The practice of Dzogchen is, properly speaking, the practice of

The distinction between what is meant by the terms *meditation* and *contemplation* in Dzogchen

contemplation, which consists in abiding in the non-dual state which, of its own nature, uninterruptedly self-liberates. This state, which is not conditioned by the conceptual level of mental activity, also encompasses thought and the functioning of what we generally consider to be our ordinary minds. Thought can, and indeed does, arise in contemplation—but, in contemplation, one is not conditioned by it; since the primordial state is inherently self-liberating, by simply leaving thought alone, it liberates of itself.

In contemplation, therefore, as the term is used in Dzogchen, the mind makes no effort whatsoever: there is nothing to do, or to abstain from doing. Since 'what is' is self-perfect just as it is, it is left in its own condition.

What is meant by 'meditation' in the Dzogchen teachings, on the other hand, is one or other of the very many practices that involve working with the dualistic, relative mind, in order to enable one to enter the state of contemplation. These practices can include the various kinds of fixation of the gaze that are done to bring one to a state of calm, as well as the various kinds of visualization practices, and so on. So, in what is called meditation, there is something to be done with the mind, but in contemplation there is not.

In Dzogchen contemplation, free from the defects of sleepiness, agitation and distraction, both the moments of calm that occur between one thought and another, and the movements of thoughts themselves are integrated in the non-dual presence of Enlightened awareness. The term *rigpa* (the opposite of *marigpa*—the fundamental delusion of dualistic mind) indicates the pure presence of this inherently self-liberating awareness, in which thought is neither rejected nor followed.

Rigpa

If one cannot find this pure presence, or rigpa, one will never find Dzogchen: to find Dzogchen, one must bring forth the naked state of rigpa. The state of rigpa is the pillar of the Dzogchen teachings, and it is this state that the master seeks to transmit in the Direct Introduction, the transmission of which, as my master Changchub Dorje showed me, is not dependent on either formal ritual initiations or intellectual explanations.

But if one does not find oneself dwelling in the state of rigpa, it is only by observing one's condition at all times that one can know just which practices to work with at any given moment in order to get out of one's cage, and to stay out of it. A bird that has lived in a cage all its life may not even know of the possibility of flight; and it will have to learn how to fly in a protected situation before it can definitively leave its cage, because otherwise, without the ability to fly well—once the bars of the cage are no longer there to protect it—it will be vulnerable to every kind of predator.

So, in the same way, a practitioner must develop mastery of his or her energies, and in the Dzogchen teachings there are practices to make this mastery possible, practices to suit all kinds of birds and all kinds of cages. But one must know for oneself what kind of bird one is, and what kind of cage one is in. And then, one must really want to come out of all cages, because it's no good just making one's cage a little bigger or more beautiful by, for example, adding some fascinating new bars made from some 'exotic' Tibetan teaching. It's no good building a new crystal cage out of the Dzogchen teachings. However beautiful it might be, it's still a cage, and the whole purpose of the Dzogchen teachings is to take one out of all cages into the expanse of the clear sky, into the space of the primordial state.

The practices of the Three Series can be classified as either 'principal practices'—non-dual contemplation itself and the practices leading to it, or as 'secondary practices'—which work **Principal** with contemplation itself in some way, or work to develop some **and second-** particular capacity. Among the secondary practices are included **ary practices** the practices known as the Six Yogas: the practice of inner heat, Tummo; the practice of the transference of consciousness, Powa; and so on,[2] as well as all the practices of levels of the teaching other than Dzogchen. Sutra practices and tantric practices of the paths of purification or transformation may be used, but they are secondary for a Dzogchen practitioner.

It must be stressed here that for the practices of Dzogchen, transmission from a master is essential. It's not that Dzogchen masters have a secret that they want to hide from others who must then try somehow or other to get it from them; the 'secret' of Dzogchen is really 'self-secret', because what is hidden from those who are in samsara is the State of Dzogchen itself, and as soon as one discovers it, it is no longer secret. But nevertheless, it must be stressed here in the strongest possible terms that in order to work with the practices of Dzogchen it is essential to have received transmission from a master, and it is also very important that there be a real commitment on the part of whoever wishes to receive specific instruction in the practices. Ideally, in fact, there should be a continuous ongoing collaboration between the master who transmits and the disciple who receives, until the transmission can be said to be complete.

Although there are an enormous variety of practices, one does not have to practice every one of them. On the contrary, one uses the practices sparingly as and when, by observing one's condition, one understands them to be useful or necessary. So here we only need to consider enough of them for a general introductory overview of the Dzogchen teachings. The reader should be aware, however, that a description of a practice is by no means the same as an instruction for that practice.

To serve as a key a table of the Three Series appears in Appendix 1. In general there are practices that work with the body, the voice, and the mind. Since each of these has become conditioned, each of these must be worked with. And so, instruction for every practice will usually include the following three elements: what the posture of the body should be, how the breathing should be, and what kind of concentration of attention, type of gaze, or form of visualization should be applied. Some practices are intended to work specifically on one of the aspects of the individual's condition, for example using control of the body and voice to focus the mind. Another practice might be aimed at simply relaxing the body, while another still might work through the voice and sound, like the *Song of the Vajra*. There are also practices using each of the elements, earth, air, fire, water, and space.

Each of the Three Series, the Semde, the Longde and the Mennagde has its own characteristic approach, but the goal is in each case the same: contemplation. And none of the Three Series is a gradual path, because in each case the master transmits directly. But the Mennagde—which literally means 'secretly spoken series', also called the Nyingthig, meaning 'heart essence' or 'essence of the essence'—is undoubtedly more direct than the Semde, which works more with oral explanation, detailed analysis, and progressive stages of meditation leading to non-dual contemplation. The Mennagde is extremely paradoxical in its introduction, because the nature of reality does not enter into the limits of logic and so cannot be explained in any other way than by paradoxes. In the Longde, on the other hand, precise positions of the body and breathing instructions lead the practitioner directly into the experience of contemplation, without the need for intellectual explanations at all.

Although the methods of presentation may vary in the Three Series, there is always a Direct Introduction in Dzogchen. It's not that there is no prior preparation, but rather that the preparation is done according to the needs of the individual. This distinguishes Dzogchen from other levels of the path in which there is a hard and fast rule which is the same for everyone. There is no need in Dzogchen for certification of one level of attainment or initiation, as is found in the gradual paths, before another higher level can be approached. Dzogchen does not work in this way. The disciple is given the opportunity to enter at the highest level right away, and only if the capacity for this level is lacking is it necessary to work down to find a level of practice that will enable whatever difficulties there may be to be overcome so that the disciple can proceed to the level of contemplation itself.

Ngondro: Preliminary Practices

In all schools of Tibetan Buddhism, not only does one normally have to proceed gradually up through all the levels of sutra and tantra, but before being allowed to practice tantra at all, one has to complete a sequence of preliminary practices, or Ngöndro, which are also known nowadays as the Four

Foundation practices. Their purpose is to develop the capacity of the individual where it is lacking, and it is absolutely correct and traditional that they are a required prerequisite for certain levels of tantric practice. I myself completed the Ngöndro twice during the course of my education. It is considered compulsory for all who wish to approach the higher practices, in all the four schools.

But Dzogchen, as the Path of Self-Liberation, approaches the situation in another way; its principle is different from that of the tantras. Garab Dorje didn't say: 'First teach the Ngöndro'. He said that the first thing to be done was for the master to introduce the disciple directly to the primordial state, so that the student would have a clear experience of it and would then have no doubts as to the fact that the state is the true condition of all phenomena. Afterwards, he said, the disciple should continue in the state, and if obstacles arose that would make this impossible, he or she should apply the specific practices necessary to overcome those obstacles: if one discovered the lack of a given capacity, one should dedicate oneself to a practice that would allow one to develop it.

Thus one can see that the principle of Dzogchen relies on the awareness of the practitioner in deciding what must be done[3], rather than on a rule compulsorily applied to one and all. This is how it must be in Dzogchen.

The Ngöndro involves practices of Refuge and Bodhichitta, the offering of the Mandala, reciting the mantra of Vajrasattva, and Guru Yoga, all of which must be carried out over 100,000 times as a preliminary to receiving higher teachings. Every level of teaching has its value and its principle, and the repetition of these practices as preliminaries truly has its function in relation to the capacity of individuals approaching the tantric teachings. In Dzogchen the same practices are carried out; but not as a preliminary to Direct Introduction, the aim being to complete them as part of the general daily pattern of practice, without a requirement to complete a certain specific number of repetitions of them. If the Ngöndro is undertaken as a preparation for tantric practice, then, for it to function, the intention of the practitioner should, in any case, never become merely that of trying to acquire a 'passport' to obtain higher teachings.

The function of the Ngöndro is to allow the disciple to purify him or herself and to accumulate merits, so that he or she may approach the Way of Wisdom, and the practice of the Ngöndro should deepen his or her commitment, make him or her more humble, increase his or her devotion toward the root-master, and, finally, allow for the surpassing of the disciple's dualistic mind in the unveiling of the state of the master in the student. If the practitioner's intention is not perfect, the Ngöndro will not fulfill its purpose; in particular, if it is undertaken with the attitude of wishing to acquire a 'passport', instead of allowing the individual to accumulate merits and to purify him or herself so that he or she may obtain wisdom, it will cause the individual to develop more pride and a false sense of superiority.

Tantric practices may be used as secondary practices by the practitioner of Dzogchen, alongside the principal practice of contemplation. All tantric practice works with visualization, but **Kyerim and** in the Inner Tantras (also called Higher or Anuttaratantras in **Dzogrim** the three later schools of Tibetan Buddhism), the practitioner must reintegrate her or his dualistic existence into the non-duality of the primordial state by using inner yogic practices as well as visualization. The process of developing the visualization is called *Kyerim*, and the work with inner yoga is called *Dzogrim*, which mean 'Development' and 'Completion' stages respectively. By means of these two stages the impure karmic vision of the individual is transformed into the pure dimension, or 'mandala', of the divinity into whose practice the master has initiated the disciple. Mantra are recited as part of this process—mantra being the natural sound of the dimension of the divinity, which thus function in practice as the vibrational key to that dimension. It is essential to receive transmission of mantra from a qualified master, or they will not function.

While physical yoga has no important role in Hinayana and Mahayana Buddhism, in Tantric Buddhism, also known as the Vajrayana (Indestructible Vehicle) or Mantrayana (Mantric

Vehicle), it is a fundamental means for realization. While the Indian form of Hatha Yoga is well known, it is not so widely appreciated that there is a specifically Tibetan form of Yoga based on the Inner Tantras (or on the Higher tantras in the schools other than the Nyingmapa).

Yantra Yoga, unlike the static Hatha Yoga, is dynamic, and works with a series of movements linked to breathing. *Trulkhor* in Tibetan, or *Yantra* in Sanskrit, means 'engine', or 'machine'. The Sanskrit term *Yoga* has been translated into Tibetan as *Naljor*, a term composed of the noun *nalwa* and the verb *jorwa*. *Nalwa* means 'the natural, unaltered state' of anything, and *jorwa* means to possess. Thus, if we put the terms *Trulkhor* and *Naljor* together, we can see that Yantra Yoga is a method for the individual to arrive at his or her natural state or condition by way of using the human body in the same way as a machine that, once set in motion, produces a specific effect.

Yantra Yoga

All of us probably have experienced how our emotions and sensations are connected to the way we breathe. A calm, deep, and relaxed regular pattern of breathing accompanies a calm and relaxed state of mind, for example, while a tense, irregular, shallow and rapid breathing pattern accompanies a state dominated by anger or hatred. Thus each mental state has its corresponding pattern of breathing, and Yantra Yoga works with the breathing to regulate the individual's energy and, ultimately, to free the mind from conditioning.

In many individuals, the body and energy are often so troubled by tensions and disturbances that even if such a person is completely dedicated to working with the mind to enter contemplation, progress is difficult. Yantra Yoga has its function as a secondary practice in Dzogchen to overcome such obstacles, and may even help the practitioner overcome physical illnesses, as specific practices of movement linked to breathing are sometimes prescribed by a Tibetan doctor as part of a cure.

It is easy to observe how various positions of the body influence one's breathing pattern. When one is seated with the trunk of the body bent double and thus closed up, the breathing will obviously be completely different from how it is when one is standing with one's arms raised above one's head and one's upper body fully open. To ensure precise control of the breathing, and thus of the energy, Yantra Yoga therefore works with movements that use the possibilities of the various positions in which the body can be placed. What is aimed at is called *natural breathing*, a way of breathing not conditioned by emotional, physical, or environmental factors.

Many tantric divinities are represented as being in union with consorts, and these forms are known as *yab-yum* (father-mother) forms. Their union represents the inseparability of relative and absolute, manifestation and voidness, method and wisdom.

The Inner Mandala

They also symbolize the union of what are called the 'solar' and 'lunar' energies, the two poles of subtle energy that flow in the subtle energy system of the human body, which is called the 'Inner Mandala'. When negative and positive circuits are joined in a lighting circuit, a lamp can be lit. When the solar and lunar energies of the subtle energy system of a human being are brought into the state of non-duality which was their inherent, latent condition from the very beginning, the human being can become illuminated. In the same way that, in the Chinese Taoist system of philosophy, Yin and Yang are seen as two principles of energy that are fundamentally inseparable and mutually interdependent constituents of a totally integrated unity, so, too, the solar and lunar energies are seen as fundamentally not-two from the very beginning. Their fundamental unity is symbolized by the Sanskrit syllable *Evam*, which is also a symbol of the *yab-yum* principle.

Karmamudra

The relationship called *karmamudra* ('action-symbol' or 'symbol of action'), the advanced yogic practice which uses sexual union as a means to achieve the union of the solar and lunar energies, is both the source and a manifestation of the yab-yum image, so prevalent in tantric ritual art, which symbolizes reality as the blissful play of voidness and energy. This relationship is a serious practice rather than being just a way to disguise eroticism as a spiritual practice or a sophisticated way to enjoy sexual contact. Its importance in the advanced stages of tantric practice can be understood from the tantric saying: 'Without Karmamudra, there is no Mahamudra'[4].

Karmamudra is not a principal practice in Dzogchen itself. In Dzogchen one integrates one's state with whatever experience one encounters, remaining in contemplation, and allowing whatever arises to self-liberate (i.e., to liberate of itself). Thus, if one does engage in sexual union, it is considered to be a valuable opportunity for practice in that the particular intensity of the sensation that arises in erotic activity can often be clearly distinguished from the state of pure presence, or rigpa, that accompanies it. But, for a Dzogchen practitioner, this way of working with sensations is not confined to the field of erotic activity.

In fact, in Dzogchen, one applies specific practices in order to create a variety of sensations, so that the practitioner is more clearly enabled to distinguish the state of presence—which always remains the same—from the sensations which change according to the practice being carried out. This obviously enables one to 'no longer remain in doubt' as to what the state of pure presence is. The practices known as the twenty-one *Semdzin* found in the Dzogchen Mennagde, or Upadesha, series, have this particular function, enabling the practitioner to separate the ordinary, reasoning mind from the nature of the mind.

The Vajra Body The 'Vajra Body' is the name given to the human body with its Inner Mandala, or subtle energy system, when it is used as a basis for practice to achieve realization. The Inner Mandala consists in three elements: the first is the structured net of vital, subtle energy-currents (which in some cases correspond to physical channels, and in some cases have no such correspondence), called *nadi* in Sanskrit and *tsa* in Tibetan; the second is the flow of vital, subtle energy through the organism, which is associated to breathing and that is called *vayu* or *prana*

The Sanskrit syllable EVAM (Calligraphy by Namkhai Norbu.)

in Sanskrit and *lung* in Tibetan; and the third is subtle energy in its essential form, which in Tibetan is called *thigle* and in Sanskrit is called *kundalini* or *bindu,* and that is not something separate from the *prana* or *lung: thigle* is the very essence of the *lung.*

It is the work done with the Inner Mandala that makes the tantric practices of the Path of Transformation a more rapid path to realization than the practices of the sutras, and there are different types of Yantra connected with the many Mahayoga tantras and their various Heruka [male wrathful yidam, see p.55 and plates 4, 7, 9 and 10] practices.

The primary function of Yantra Yoga is to gain mastery of the prana, the vital energy of the body, by means of a series of movements, or Yantra, that are linked to the breathing process to control, coordinate, and develop it; and to activate the thigle, or kundalini, the vital essence, by means of *asana*, or positions linked to movement. It is from the Inner Mandala, or subtle energy system, that the physical body develops. In the process of conception the flow of subtle energy animates and develops the fertilized physical ovum in the womb of the mother, and then causes the development of the embryo and, later, the fetus; thus the correct development of the fetus depends on the proper flow of subtle energy. Similarly, throughout life of the individual, health depends on the correct circulation of prana and the balance of the elements. A secondary function of Yantra Yoga can therefore be in helping to keep the individual healthy.

According to Tantra there are 72,000 subtle channels in the Inner Mandala; there are main channels, and lesser channels, which branch and interconnect in a pattern like a tree that has **Channels** a main trunk, with roots and branches spreading out from it **and Chakras** into finer and finer configurations. The points where the subtle channels come together, like spokes coming into a hub, are called *chakras* in Sanskrit, or *khorlo* in Tibetan. There are very many of these, but the principal ones are found along the central channel, which is like the main trunk of the tree in the analogy above. The essence of prana, kundalini, or thigle concentrates in these principal chakras, in a subtle channel within the spinal

Padmasambhava as Guru Amitayus, in union with his consort. The Buddha Amitayus—an emanation of the Buddha Amitabha—is the Buddha of Long Life; the manifestation of Padmasambhava pictured here is visualized in practices undertaken to strengthen the life-force of the practitioner and thus increase the individual's life-span for the purpose of having more time to attain realization. Both the Guru and his consort hold in their right hands a dadar *or arrow with a mirror or* melong *and five-color ribbons which absorb the energy of the five elements, and in their left hands, a long-life vase. In general, yab-yum forms symbolize the bliss of realization, the play of energy which manifests from the voidness of the Base, and the essential inseparability of pleasure and voidness. (Line drawing by Nigel Wellings.)*

column, called the Gyungpa. At the navel chakra sixty-four channels connect; at the heart chakra, eight; at the throat chakra, sixteen; and at the head chakra, thirty-two.

In general, it is said that the central channel—*kundarma* or *uma*—is flanked by two further major channels, to the right and left of it, which are respectively called *roma* and *kyangma* or 'solar channel' and 'lunar channel', which unite with the central channel in the lower part of the trunk and which then run parallel to it up the body, arching at the top over the cranium, before turning down to link up with the right and left nostrils. These three principal channels are shown in the details from the murals from the Fifth Dalai Lama's secret temple, to be found among the plates included in this book.

Various tantras give instructions for practice using different numbers of chakras. This doesn't mean, however, that there is an inconsistency between them; the tantras are in agreement as to the nature of the subtle energy system. But since different practices have specific and varying aims, different channels and chakras are put into function to achieve those aims, and in the description of any given practice only the particular channels and chakras specific to that practice are described. If this is not understood it may seem that different tantras contradict each other[5].

Since prana and the mind are linked, prana follows the mind when guided by concentration; prana gathers when the mind focuses it. And conversely, the mind can be balanced and integrated by working with the prana through the use of controlled breathing patterns and movements that are linked to breathing. There are many types of prana, and they support the many types of dualistic mind; as long as the prana circulates in the many and various channels, these dualistic minds persist. But when the prana is brought into the central channel, its essential nature—thigle, or kundalini—is activated and enters the channels. Dualistic mind is then overcome, and realization achieved. The vital energy will not normally enter the central channel except at the time of death or during sleep. Only practice will otherwise cause it to do so. Although various tantras specify different chakras at which the prana should be induced to enter the central channel, they all specify that it should be brought to enter there.

There are 108 practices of the 'Union of the Solar and Lunar' Yantra, including five loosening exercises to prepare the muscles and channels, five practices, or purification and loosening joints; eight principal movements; five principal groups of five positions; fifty variations on the twenty-five positions; seven lotuses; and the Wave of the Vajra, which corrects all errors of practice.

These 108 practices also include the nine purification breathings which are always practiced before a session of Yantra Yoga to expel all the impure air from the system, and are also very beneficial before a session of meditation of any kind; and the rhythmic breathing which serves to steady and deepen the breathing, and to develop the capacity for holding the breath which is used in *kumbhaka*, a particular type of closed holding in which the air is subtly pressed down in the abdominal region, without disturbing the stomach, while at the same time it is pulled up from below, focusing and concentrating the prana, before causing it to enter the central channel.

The eight principal movements, or yantra, are a linked series of movements, each of which serves to guide and guarantee a particular type of breathing. By linking the breathing to movement, correct timing is guaranteed, and the various positions into which the body is moved ensure that the type of breathing is accurate in each case. The eight types of breathing are as follows: Slow Inhaling; Open Holding; *Shil* (or pushing down); Rapid Exhalation; Rapid Inhalation; Closed Holding; Dren (drawing); and Slow Exhalation. Each of the eight movements have seven phases of breathing.

The five principal groups of five positions, or asanas, each work to develop and stabilize a particular aspect of the breathing, combining the eight types of breathing with five methods for causing the prana to enter the central channel. The practitioner does not have to master all of the twenty-five positions, but one from each group is sufficient, depending on the capacity of

ཨྃ༔ ཁ་ཡར་མ་ཡུང་རང་གི་ལུགས་ལུང་རང་ༀ ཟྲིག་ཟྲིག་ཏད་མྱྀན་པའི་ཙྩ་ཚོགས།
རཔ་ཧྲུ་མ་པ༔ ཟྲུ་སྩྀ་ྒྱྀ་ནས་མྱྀ་མར་ཡྀ་ཡི་ལ་སྩྱུ་ནད་པྲུ༔ ཡེ་རྀ་ཚྀ་ན་ཞྀ་ནར་ནས་ལ
ཟྲ་ག་ར་ཚྀ་ཡུར་ྱྀ ༔

*Vairochana. The particular tradition of Yantra Yoga that I teach does not
belong to the Vajrayana, or Tantra, but to Atiyoga or Dzogchen, and it was
one of the first to be introduced to Tibet. It is connected with the Heruka
Ngondzog Gyalpo, and is known as the 'Union of the Solar and Lunar'
Yantra[6]. Its title refers to the reintegration of the solar and lunar energies
of the subtle energy system. It was written down by Vairochana, the great
Tibetan translator who was a disciple of Padmasambhava and Humkara[7], in
the eighth century C.E., and from that time until the present day there has
continued an uninterrupted lineage of transmission of it, in Kham, eastern
Tibet. It was summarized and extensively taught by Adzam Drugpa, from
whose direct disciples I received transmission and instruction. (Tibetan
wood-block print, artist unknown.)*

the individual and the condition of his or her body. Each of the asanas has seven phases of breathing.

Yantra Yoga is a secondary practice. That is to say, it belongs to the group of practices that help one to gain access to the state of contemplation, or allow one to work with contemplation towards some particular capacity, or to achieve some specific aim, such as healing oneself or others. The reciting of mantras, the visualization of divinities, all the practices of purification, or of transformation, may be used by a practitioner of Dzogchen, but their use is secondary to the practice of contemplation. A practitioner of Dzogchen is not limited, and can draw from any source that is useful, whenever needed. But, naturally, the practitioner is not in the least interested in making a collection of different paths and traditions, or practices. When one functions on the relative plane all one's actions must be governed by a relative awareness that distinguishes clearly between what is useful and what is merely distraction.

Secondary Practices

People often tell me that they are not interested in ritual practices, only in meditation or contemplation. But while it is true that ritual practices are secondary to the practice of contemplation in Dzogchen, nevertheless, through concentration, mantra, and mudra, a practitioner can have contact with energy in a very real and concrete way. I can perhaps most easily show what I mean by this by including here a story about something that happened during the long journey I made when I left Tibet for India as the political situation in my native country steadily deteriorated and I grew certain that a great upheaval was soon to occur.

The use of ritual

I was travelling on horseback from eastern to central Tibet in a party of four families that included about thirty people. Because of the presence of the Chinese troops, we didn't make use of the normal roads, but travelled by secondary routes. On these there was further danger from the many bandits who were taking advantage of the confusion of the times to rob groups of travellers. We had many valuable horses, and between the danger from the bandits and the Chinese troops, our journey was very difficult.

At a certain point we knew that bandits were following us, and we had two skirmishes with them. In the first they succeeded in stealing some of our horses, and in the second we captured two of the bandits. We learned from these two prisoners that their friends were planning to attack us in force, but we didn't know when, and in the middle of the vast open plain through which we were passing there was nowhere to hide. I felt that the only thing to do was to summon the help of the Guardians of the teaching, and so whenever we stopped to eat or rest I would go into a little tent, and for hours I would practice a rite invoking them.

The danger increased daily, and a few days later, as I became more deeply involved in this practice, something strange began to happen. I seemed to see sparks coming from the big ritual drum as I sounded it. At first I thought it must be a problem with my eyes, a hallucination, or perhaps some freak of friction between the stick and the drum, but when I called my sister, she too saw the sparks in the air around the drum. Then I called my brother, and later my parents and the whole of our party, and they all saw the sparks. We were sure that it was a sign that the bandits would attack that night, and so we tied the horses up away from the camp, while everyone stayed awake all night on guard and ready for action. But no bandits came, and when I practiced the next day, the sparks were there as before. They continued to manifest day after day for nearly a week as we travelled, but then one day there were no sparks. This time we were certain the bandits would come, and we prepared our defenses with great care. Sure enough, we were attacked by a whole band of them. But surprise was on our side, and we were able to drive them off without casualty to our group. From then on they left us alone, and we travelled safely to central Tibet. So you see, even secondary practices can bring very definite advantages.

Guardians of the Teachings

There are eight principal classes of Guardians each with many subdivisions. Some are highly realized beings, others not realized at all. Every place—every continent, country, city, mountain, river, lake or forest—has its particular dominant energy, or Guardian, as have every year, hour and even minute: these are not highly evolved energies. The various teachings all have energies which have special relationships with them: these are more realized Guardians. These energies are iconographically portrayed as they were perceived when they manifested to masters who had contact with them, and their awesome power is represented by their terrifyingly ferocious forms, their many arms and heads, and their ornaments of the charnel ground. As with all the figures in tantric iconography, it is not correct to interpret the figures of the guardians as merely symbolic, as some Western writers have been tempted to do. Though the iconographic forms have been shaped by the perceptions and culture of those who saw the original manifestation and by the development of tradition, actual beings are represented.

Principal Practices

The Semde practices of *shiné*, involving fixation to bring one into a state of calm, and *lhagthong*, enabling one to dissolve the mental activity of maintaining that state of calm so that one can work with the arising of thought, are practices of meditation rather than of contemplation. They are nevertheless considered to be principal practices, as they serve to bring one into contemplation; but they are not of themselves the actual practice of Dzogchen, because practice becomes truly Dzogchen only when it reaches the level of non-dual contemplation. Indeed, practices of Semde and Longde, though not exactly the same as those found in the Semde, are to be found in almost all Buddhist schools.

Once the state of non-dual contemplation has been arrived at, by whatever means, from whichever of the Three Series, one will have the taste of it oneself, and one will no longer be in any doubt as to what it is. Then one must continue in it. This continuation has two levels of practice, *Tregchöd* and *Thödgal*, both principal practices, which are presented in the Mennagde.

The Mennagde is, however, not something only to be practiced after the practices of the Semde and the Longde. It is, on the contrary, a complete teaching in itself that has its own secondary practices of purification and preparation among

Rushen

The Twenty-
one Principal
Semdzin

Tregchöd
and Thödgal

which are to be found the *Rushen,* whose aim is to enable us to distinguish the mind from the nature of the mind, 'separating' them; and the twenty-one principal *Semdzin,* which work with a whole range of methods, including fixation, breathing, different body postures, sounds, and so on, to bring one into the state of contemplation.

Once one has arrived at contemplation through any method, one has to continue in it, and working to bring this continuation into every action and situation is called *Tregchöd,* which literally means '(spontaneous) cutting of tension', in the sense that as soon as the primordial state manifests and dualism is thus overcome, one instantly falls into a state of total relaxation, like a bundle of sticks, that, having been tightly bound together, falls loosely into a totally relaxed pattern as soon as the string binding it has been cut.

Continuing beyond Tregchöd there is the practice of Thödgal, which means 'surpassing the utmost', with the sense that 'as soon as you're here, you're there'. This practice is genuinely secret, and it is not appropriate to give more than the most basic description of it here. This is not the same as an instruction for practice. Thödgal is found only in the Dzogchen teachings. Through the practice of it one is able to carry one's state of being rapidly to the ultimate goal.

Through the development of the Four Lights, the Four Visions of Thödgal arise, and working with the inseparability of vision and emptiness one proceeds until the realization of the Body of Light is attained. This is the consummation of existence in which the physical body itself is dissolved into the essence of the elements, which is light. I shall discuss this later, when we come to the section of this book that deals with the 'Fruit', or realization. But for the practice of Thödgal to function, the practice of Tregchöd must first be perfect, and the practitioner must be able to remain in the state of contemplation at all times.

Although I, for example, had received instructions on the practice of Thödgal from Changchub Dorje when I was with him in Tibet, it was not until many years later that I actually began to put it into practice. I simply did not think that I had developed sufficient capacity. But one night, after I had already been living and teaching at University in Italy many years, I had a dream in which, as often happened in my dreams, I returned to visit my master Changchub Dorje in Tibet. On this occasion my master greeted me and said: 'Ah, so you've comeback from Italy then, have you?' And I replied: 'Yes, but I have to go back there again right away.' I said this because I was a bit worried about what would happen if the Chinese authorities found me in Tibet without a permit.

Then my master asked me how my practice was progressing. I said that I thought it was going well enough, and he asked: 'What practice have you been doing the most?' 'Still the Tregchöd,' I replied. 'Still concentrating on the Tregchöd!' he exclaimed. 'Haven't you begun to practice Thödgal yet?' I replied that I hadn't, reminding him that he himself had always told me that it was necessary to become well established in the Tregchöd first. 'Yes,' he said, 'but I didn't say that you should spend your whole life practicing it; now it's time for you to practice Thödgal. If you have any doubts about it, go and ask Jigmed Lingpa.' I thought that this was a very strange thing to say because I knew, of course, that Jigmed Lingpa was a great Dzogchen master of the eighteenth century who had been dead for many years. I thought perhaps I had misunderstood what my master had said, so I asked him to explain, but he just said: 'Jigmed Lingpa is up on the mountain behind the house. Go and see him right away.'

Behind the house where my master lived there was a high rocky mountain, and he told me that I should climb to the top of it to a place where there was a cave in which I would find Jigmed Lingpa. But this instruction puzzled me, because I already knew that mountain quite well, as I'd climbed it many times to gather medicinal herbs while I lived with my master, and during all that time I had never seen a cave there. So I thought: 'Well that's very strange—I don't think there's a cave there at all,' but what I said out loud was: 'Which of the paths up the mountain should

I take to get up to this cave?', because, in fact, there were two ways up the mountain.

But the master just said: 'Climb straight up from here! Go on, just do it right away! And when you find Jigmed Lingpa, ask him to clear up any doubts you may have about Thödgal. Then practice it.'

I wanted to ask him some more questions but I knew that it was impossible, because the master could get quite wrathful if provoked, and I was afraid he might scold me if I persisted. So I said: 'All right; I'll go at once.'

Then, in my dream I climbed up the mountain directly behind the house. There was no path there, and the rock face was fairly smooth, but I managed to clamber up it. At a certain point I noticed that there were what at first seemed to be mantras carved into the rock in the typical way that Tibetans often inscribe them on such surfaces. But then, when I looked more closely to see what kind of mantras they might be, I saw that they were not mantras at all. I read a few sentences of the carved words and discovered that what was written there was in fact a whole Tantra, a Tantra of Dzogchen, it seemed to me. So then I thought: 'This is not a very good action! I'm walking on a Tantra!' and I began to recite the hundred-syllable mantra of Vajrasattva to purify my negative action, as I continued climbing.

At that point I arrived at a large boulder that stood up out of the rock face, and I found that the title of a Tantra was written quite clearly on it. I later discovered, in my waking life, that this title was the name of a *terma* (or hidden treasure) of the Upadesha, or Mennagde series of the Dzogchen teachings. But in my dream that night I went on climbing beyond this boulder until I came to a flat meadow, at the far side of which I could see a large rocky outcrop. I walked slowly over to these rocks, and searching around among them, to my great surprise, I really did find a cave. And then, even though I still wasn't fully convinced that Jigmed Lingpa would be inside, I cautiously made my way into the cave mouth.

Once inside, I looked around me and saw that the cave was quite large—large enough, in fact, for there to be a big white rock in the middle of it. And on this rock there sat a child—a very small, young child—who was wearing pale blue clothing made of a diaphanous material similar to that from which some kinds of ladies' nightgowns are made in the West. The child had very long hair, and he was sitting quite normally, with his legs stretched out in front of him, not in a meditation or practice position. I climbed up onto the big white rock and looked to the left and right to see if anyone else might be there, but there was no one else in the cave.

I thought to myself: 'This can't possibly be Jigmed Lingpa, because this is only a very young child,' and I slowly went nearer to him. The child seemed just as amazed to see me as I was to see him. Then, since my master had specifically sent me to meet Jigmed Lingpa and there was no one else in the cave, I decided that this must be him, and that I shouldn't be disrespectful. So, as the child still continued just gazing at me, I said with great respect: 'My master has sent me to find you.' The child then, with a sign—but still without speaking—indicated that I should sit down. Since he didn't speak, I didn't say anything more either, but as I sat down I was wondering to myself what on Earth he might do next.

And what he did in fact do was to put his hand up to his head—his long hair wasn't tied up in any special way, but just hung loose—and pull out a piece of rolled up paper that looked a bit like half a cigarette. Then he open this little scroll of paper and began reading aloud from it. I was surprised that his voice really was the voice of a child, but as he read it became clear to me that what he was reading was a Tantra, and I thought to myself: 'So there really was something in what my master said when he told me to come up here and find Jigmed Lingpa!'—the words he was reading were all about the Four Lights of Thödgal. I was really amazed, and at that moment I woke up and found myself in my familiar apartment in Italy. I knew then that it was time for me to begin to practice Thödgal.

Signs of this kind often manifest from one's own clarity when one's master is not present to give instructions or advice in person, but it is important not to confuse fantasy with real clarity. Fantasy is impure vision and arises from karmic traces in the conditioned stream of consciousness of the individual, whereas clarity is a manifestation of pure vision. To begin the practice of Thödgal prematurely, or at the wrong time, without sufficient development of Tregchöd, will certainly cause serious obstacles on the path. The best safeguard against this is the guidance of a qualified master, and complete confidence in his instructions on the part of the disciple

Dzogchen is considered a very high teaching, containing as it does practices that lead so directly to such complete realization as the Body of Light. Indeed, no one, in any of the Buddhist schools, denies that Dzogchen is a high teaching, even the highest. But what they do say is that it is too high—in fact, beyond the capacity of ordinary people—and they speak of it almost as if it were only to be practiced by realized beings. But if a being is truly realized, he or she has no need of a path at all.

Beginning on the Path

According to the texts of Dzogchen itself, there are just five capacities that someone must have to be able to practice Dzogchen, and if one examines oneself and finds that these five are not missing, then nothing is missing. And if any of the capacities is lacking, then one can set about working to develop it. But in most people they will probably already be present.

Five capacities necessary for the practice of Dzogchen

Participation

This means that one must have a desire to hear and understand the teaching. But more than this, it means that one actively gives one's full cooperation to participating with the master. It is not just that the master explains, and there is nothing required on the part of the disciple.

Diligence

This means that one must be consistent in one's participation, and not waver in one's commitment, changing one's mind from day to day, continually putting off doing something.

Jigmed Lingpa (1729-98) was a great Dzogchen master of the Nyingmapa school who lived in eastern Tibet. He was a reincarnation of Vimalamitra, the great eighth-century Dzogchen master who became the official teacher of the Tibetan king Trisong Deutsen. Jigmed Lingpa brought to fruition the renaissance of the teachings begun by Longchen Rabjampa (1308-63), of whom he had many visions throughout his life. He never undertook any formal academic studies, but, upon completing a solitary retreat of five years, manifested such wide knowledge through his clarity that he came to be universally regarded as a great scholar. He edited and compiled the Longchen Nyingthig and left nine volumes of collected works, including authoritative writings on Tibetan history and medicine, and a text on the curative properties of gem stones when worn next to the skin. He inspired the development of the 'Rimed' or ecumenical, movement that arose in eastern Tibet to draw the various schools of Tibetan Buddhism into a more harmonious collaboration as sectarianism was deepening the divisions among them. (Tibetan wood-block print, artist unknown.)

ཨྠ། །བཀྲལ་པབརུང་ནགཆ་ཚུབས་པའི་ཏེ་ཊྲི་ལགོཡི་རྣགལ། །ཁབ་མདང་ལེ་ཤེ་རྩོ་གགལ་ཎྚེ་ཀྀ་མོ་ནེ། །

མཁོ་འི་དབང་ཕྱུག་ཎྡྲེ་དཔའི་རྒྱལ་མོ་ཆེ། །ཕྱག་སརྤ་དགར་རལ་མ་ཚེག་མ་པ་ཕྲུ་ནག་ཚོ་ལྷྀ་ཕྱོ། །

*Ekajati, whose name means 'One Single Birth', is the principal Guardian
of the Dzogchen teachings. She manifests with one single eye, one single
tooth, one single tuft of hair, and one single breast. A personification of
the essentially non-dual nature of primordial energy, she does not allow
duality to develop. She is seen dancing on the corpse of the conquered ego,
wearing (as Simhamukha does) a flayed human skin, and a crown of five
skulls representing the five passions that have been overcome and which can
therefore be worn as ornaments. She wears a necklace of human skulls, and
wields in one hand, as a scepter, the corpse of a perverter of the teachings. In
the other hand she grasps a vanquished demon, and the heart of an enemy.
(Tibetan wood-block print, artist unknown.)*

ཨྰོཾ། །ཁྱུང་ལག་ཏེ་གི་སྐུངས་སམས་རཔ་རབ་ད། །སྐུ་བ་དྲུང་ནེ་སམས་མ་འཇོར་ནོ་བས་ཀྲུག་པ་ལམེ །
འཛོམ་སྒུལ་སྒུལ་རོ་རབ་གག་ལེ་རུ་རའེ་ད། །སྐོ་ལམ་གི་རྡོ་རྗེ་ལེ་གས་སར་རྦུ་གས་ཚོ་ལམ་ནོ །

This Tibetan wood-block print shows Dorje Legpa, another of the principal Guardians of Dzogchen, mounted on a lion. He is also often shown mounted on a goat. Dorje Legpa, which means 'Good Vajra', was a Guardian and he manifested to oppose Padmasambhava's efforts to establish the Buddhist teachings in Tibet.

Padmasambhava conquered him and bound him by oath to protect the teachings. He is thus sometimes known as the 'Oath-Bound One'. As his energy is less overwhelming than that of Rahula, he can be approached for assistance with relatively mundane matters, while Ekajati and Rahula are only concerned with matters strictly relating to the teachings and realization. (Artist unknown.)

The Guardians of the Mahakala class are the principal Guardians of many teachings. They are secondary Guardians of the Dzogchen teachings. There are very many types of Mahakala, governed by a principal Mahakala, Maning. The Mahakalas are male; though there are also feminine Mahakalis, they are under the dominance of the Mahakalas. Only the Dzogchen teachings, in which the feminine principle of energy is of such prime importance, have a feminine protector, Ekajati, as the principal Guardian. (Tibetan wood-block print, artist unknown.)

ཨོཾ། །བཀའ་འཛིན་རྒྱུད་གཉིས་ཀྱི་བལྟ་ངན་རྣམ་རྣམ། དུག་གདོང་ཏྲིག་ལས་པ་བཞིན་འའི་མ་ཡོའམ་པོའི། །
དུག་གདུང་སྲུང་གཉིས་ནི་སྟུག་ཏྲིག་ངར་བར། །ཁལ་རྩུ་ལྔ་རྒྱས་གཏུག་གིན་ཅེ་ངོ་ཏྲུ་གར་ཙ་རྣམ། །

Rahula is another of the principal Guardians of the Dzogchen teachings. His lower body is like that of a snake, while his upper body is covered with eyes, which, together with the further eyes in his nine heads symbolize his ability to see in all directions. His bow and arrow are ready to strike at enemies, and his mouths are ready to devour their ignorance.

He is shown in this wood-block print surrounded by flames of high energy, as are all Guardians, but Rahula's power is so intense that, unless the practitioner has already developed considerable mastery, he can be a dangerous ally of potentially overwhelming power if not approached in the right way. (Tibetan wood-block print, artist unknown.)

Present Awareness

This means that one must not become distracted. One must remain present in the moment, every moment. It is no good knowing all the theory of the teaching, but still living distractedly just the same.

Actual practice

One must actually enter into contemplation. It is not sufficient just to know how to practice, one must actually enter into practice. This is to enter into the Way of Wisdom.

Prajña

In the absolute sense, this Sanskrit word means 'super-knowledge' or 'knowledge which goes beyond'. In this case, however, the condition indicated by the term is mainly relative and it indicates the possession of the necessary intellectual capacity to understand whatever one is taught, although it also implies the presence of the capacity of *insight* necessary to directly grasp what is pointed at beyond words, and then to effectively enter into the dimension of transcendent knowledge that the words are pointing to. This way one gains access to wisdom itself.

This 'transcendent knowledge' or prajña: is not, of course, just an intellectual knowledge. As I have often repeated, my master Changchub Dorje for example never received an intellectual education; yet his wisdom and the qualities that arose from it were nevertheless quite remarkable. He would sit every day in the enclosed courtyard in front of his house to receive those who came to see him for spiritual or medical advice. He had never actually studied medicine, but his medical knowledge had manifested spontaneously from the great clarity that had arisen from his state of contemplation, and such was his skill as a healer that people came from far and wide to be treated by him. I learned about this clarity first hand through participating in a process that was another extraordinary manifestation of it.

After I had been only a few days with Changchub Dorje, he asked me to take dictation from him. I knew that he could not read and write, and as I can write well enough, I naturally agreed to be of what service I could, without thinking too much of it. I would sit inside the house at a table, and through the one open pane of a window made of four panes of horn I could both see and hear the master outside in the courtyard, where he was usually busy with his patients and disciples. In the middle of all the bustle of activity that surrounded him he would begin to dictate to me, without even a moment's hesitation about what he was going to say. Then he would stop dictating, all the while carrying on with his work, while I finished writing down what he had said. When I was done, I would call out that I'd finished. He would break off talking to those who had come to see him and, without a pause, would begin dictating some more lines, sometimes prose, sometimes verse. But he never once had to ask: 'Now where was I?', 'Where did we stop?', or anything like that. On the contrary, it was often me who had to ask him to repeat something he had said that I had forgotten. As we proceeded like this for the first few days I was convinced, as I was writing, that the various fragmentary pieces that he was dictating would never assume an overall shape that would form proper paragraphs and chapters. But every night I would go back to my room and read through what I had written down in the disjointed way in which I had received the dictation, and I always found that the whole thing flowed along with a complete continuity just like a perfectly conceived and written intellectual text; this is in fact exactly the way in which '*Gongter*' [mind terma] always manifests. Over the next weeks we completed a big volume working in this way, and I later saw some of the twenty other such volumes that had been similarly dictated to his other disciples.

> All that arises
> is essentially no more real
> than a reflection,
> transparently pure and clear,
> beyond all definition
> or logical explanation.

> Yet the seeds of past action,
> karma, continue to cause
> further arising.

> Even so,
> know that all that exists
> is ultimately void of self-nature,
> utterly non-dual!

These words of the Buddha are a perfect explanation of Dzogchen.

Chödpa: Conduct, or Attitude

The last of the three aspects of the Path is *Chödpa*, which means 'Conduct', or 'Attitude' and this is a very important aspect of Dzogchen because this is the way practice is brought into daily life so that there is no separation between practice and whatever activity one engages in.

The absolute, spontaneous, non-dual awareness of the primordial state, experienced in contemplation, is self-perfected and thus beyond all effort. In this state there is nothing to practice, nothing that must be done, and nothing that cannot be done. But whenever the individual is not in the state of contemplation, effort must be applied to recognize this fact and to bring about a return to contemplation.

Until one is able to live in contemplation—in the self-perfected state in which thoughts and passions are 'like a thief in an empty house'— one has to train oneself not to become distracted, and to govern one's conduct with awareness—in this case an awareness that requires the provisional application of effort, through which one trains oneself to develop the non-dual, effortless awareness of the primordial state. We have already seen that this kind of awareness maintained through applying effort is one of the five capacities necessary to practice Dzogchen; unless one is the kind of exceptional being for whom the primordial state arises spontaneously, one must at first make an effort to really be present and mindful in every moment.

But once this mindfulness is established, the Dzogchen practitioner can develop this present awareness in daily life so that what would otherwise be the 'poison' of dualistic experience itself becomes the path to remain in contemplation beyond dualism. In the same way that flowing water freezes into solid ice, the free flow of primordial energy is solidified by the action of conditioned cause and effect—the functioning of the individual's karma—into a seemingly concrete material world. The 'great perfection' of the practitioner's attitude, or Chödpa, makes possible the mastery of karmic causes, so that they self-liberate as they arise.

For any action of body, voice, or mind to become a perfect primary karmic cause capable of conditioning the individual and producing a full karmic consequence all these three aspects must occur: first there must be an intention to act; then the action itself must be carried out; and finally, there must be satisfaction at having performed the action.

Primary karmic causes, good or bad, are like seeds which are capable of reproducing the species of plant from which they came. But just as seeds need secondary causes such as light, moisture, and air if they are to mature, so too the primary karmic **Primary and secondary karmic causes** causes remaining as the traces of past actions in the stream of consciousness of the individual need secondary causes if they are to be able to mature into further actions and situations of the same kind. By means of continual awareness the practitioner can work with the secondary causes arising as the conditions he or she encounters in daily life so that the primary causes of samsara are prevented from coming into fruition, while at the same time whatever is conducive to liberation is furthered, until finally he or she becomes so firmly established in the primordial state that it is impossible to be conditioned by any experience that may arise, good or bad, and the practitioner may be said to have attained total liberation from conditioned existence altogether.

A practitioner can develop beyond the dualistic level of **Three factors necessary to produce a primary karmic cause** conditioned karma that divides things into good and bad, and may thus be able to do all kinds of things that seem outrageous from the divisive dualistic point of view of ordinary karmic vision. But this kind of 'authentic behavior' is not the same at all as remaining distractedly caught up in dualism and just doing

The author's principal master, Changchub Dorje, is shown here seated in the enclosed courtyard of his house in Derghe, eastern Tibet, waiting to receive patients or other visitors. He wears the robes of a layman and a traditional melong, a mirror made of five precious metals, symbol of Dzogchen, on a cord around his neck. On the table in front of him are small bags of medicine, a measuring spoon and medicine bowl. Behind him, to the right, are two larger sacks of medicine, and above them, glimpsed through the open window, the author sits at a table inside, ready to take dictation. Prayer flags flutter above. (Line drawing by Nigel Wellings.)

whatever comes into your head. That kind of distracted behavior would be the most extreme violation of the ideal of Dzogchen, the Great Perfection—the practice of non-dual contemplation that manifests in a spontaneous life in which the play of one's own energies can be fully enjoyed. Nor does everyone who practices Dzogchen have to live like the famous Tibetan crazy-wisdom yogi, Drugpa Kunleg[8], who was beyond dualism, and beyond all limits, and who therefore never behaved as others expected—so that dozens of interesting stories are told of him to this day, many of them hilariously bawdy.

Dzogchen is not mere license; when the practitioner does not find him or herself in the non-dual state of contemplation, he or she has the commitment to uninterruptedly maintain the presence of awareness—awareness in this case meaning the type of attention that is aware of the effects and consequences of one's actions. As has already been noted, though, this is not the same as living by rules: awareness replaces all rules and becomes the only rule in Dzogchen, for a Dzogchen practitioner never forces him or herself to do something and never submits her or himself to being conditioned by anything 'external'.

This doesn't mean, though, that a Dzogchen practitioner shows no respect for the rules by which other people live. One doesn't just go around being contrary to everyone else, using Dzogchen to justify one's strange actions. Both the effortless non-dual awareness of rigpa that is the ideal for a Dzogchen practitioner, and the 'relative awareness' that we make an effort to maintain when we recognize that we are not in the state of contemplation, involve us in being aware of everything—including, of course, the needs of other people. Because, even if the absolute condition is beyond good and evil, the relative condition nevertheless still continues to exist for us as long as we remain conditioned by dualism, and we have to be aware of that, too. But we can live respecting the conditions which exist around us without getting bound up in them. This is the principle of the attitude, or Chödpa, of a Dzogchen practitioner.

One must not become conditioned by the teachings themselves. The teachings are there to make one more independent, not more dependent. So a Dzogchen master will always be trying to help the disciple to become more truly autonomous, to come out of all cages, completely. And thus, while the master is certainly able, out of his or her greater clarity, to give advice to disciples, even on quite detailed matters relating to everyday life, he or she will always be trying to help them to observe themselves, and to make decisions out of their own awareness.

Masters can, of course, just as well be women as men. When I was fourteen, I myself spent two months with the great woman master Ayu Khandro, who lived a few days ride away from my college. As she was considered to have realized the practice of Vajrayogini, and thus to be an embodiment of this dakini, I was sent during a break in my college studies to ask her for the Vajrayogini initiation. She was a very aged woman, not at all well-known, who had lived for more than fifty years in a small house in total darkness working with a practice known as the *Yangthig*, which enables someone who is already able to remain in the state of contemplation to proceed to total realization through the development of inner luminosity and visionary clarity.

Yangthig

When I arrived at Ayu Khandro's house it became clear that she could see as well in the dark as she could in the light. Although her attendant lit a few butter lamps for my benefit, I was aware that Ayu Khandro herself had no need of them. By the light of the lamps I saw the features of this very striking old woman. Her long hair, which hung down well below her waist in plaited braids, was gray from its roots to below her shoulders, but from there on it was black to its tips. It had clearly never been cut. At first Ayu Khandro declined to give me the initiation I requested, saying she was just a poor old woman who knew nothing about the teachings, but she did suggest that we camp nearby for the night. During the night she had an auspicious dream in which her master urged her to give me the initiation, and so, in the morning she sent her attendant with breakfast for my mother and sister, and an invitation for me to go to see her. In the following weeks she transmitted a great deal of teaching to me, including the complete practice of the Yangthig, and I regard her as one of my principal masters. During my stay with her, in response to my questions, she told me her life story, which I later wrote down[9].

So, the Chöpa or conduct of the Dzogchen practitioner consists in remaining constantly and uninterruptedly in the state of absolute presence or non-dual contemplation, not allowing the mind to wander after thoughts about the past, worries about the present, or plans for the future. If dualistic mind arises and interrupts one's state of contemplation, and if one cannot immediately recover the state, then one should maintain the presence of the kind of relative awareness that clearly recognizes the consequences of one's actions and relates them to the principles of the teachings. Every time we find ourselves in the relative, dualistic plane we should maintain this presence.

This does not mean that one should not make any plans at all, but rather that one should remain aware of secondary causes as they arise and—unlike the father of 'Famous Moon', the unfortunate hero of a Tibetan story that aptly illustrates what may happen when one is not present—one should relate to secondary causes in a way that is free of attachment and aversion, hope and fear, and all the conflicted neurotic entanglements of deluded mind.

The story tells that there was once a man so poor that the only way he could get something to eat was to go from door to door asking others more fortunate than himself to give him some grain. One day he was lucky; he received a great deal of grain, and he went home happy. His house was very small indeed, and since there were so many mice in it, he decided to hang his precious grain in a sack suspended by a rope from the roof beam, so that the mice couldn't get at it. Then he lay down for the night on his bed, which was below the sack, there being so little room in the house. He couldn't get to sleep right away, so he began to make plans in his mind. He thought to himself: 'I won't eat all the grain in my sack; I'll save some of it for seed, plant it, and then grow more grain. In a year I'll have ten sacks, and the year after that I'll have a hundred.' And he went on planning how year after year he'd have more sacks until he was rich, and then he thought: 'I won't have to live in this tiny little hut any more, I'll build myself a palace and have servants to look after me. I'll find myself a beautiful wife, and then of course well have children. We'll have a son first, I'm sure, but what on earth shall we call him?' And he lay there trying to think of a name for his future son. He thought of many names, but none of them pleased him. Finally, a clear bright moon rose in the black sky, and as soon as he saw it he exclaimed to himself: 'That's it! I'll call him 'Famous Moon'!' But at that precise moment a mouse that had been gnawing at the rope that held the sack of grain tied to the beam above him finally cut through the rope with his teeth, and the sack fell on the poor man's head, killing him instantaneously, so that none of his elaborate plans ever came to be. Living in dreams of the future, even the present escaped him.

Chapter 8

The Fruit

> If the intention is good,
> the Path and the Fruit will be good.
>
> If the intention is bad,
> the Path and the Fruit will be bad.
>
> Since everything thus
> depends on a good intention,
>
> always strive to cultivate
> such a positive mental attitude.
>
> —*Jigmed Lingpa*

The divisions of the teaching of Dzogchen are for the purposes of explanation only. Realization is not something that must be constructed; to become realized simply means to discover and manifest that which from the very beginning has been our own true condition: the Zhi (gzhi) or Base. And, in particular, in Dzogchen—which not a gradual Path—the Path consists in remaining in the unveiled, manifest condition of the primordial state or Base, or in other words, in the condition which is the Fruit. This is why the Gankyil, the symbol of primordial energy, which is a particular symbol of the Dzogchen teachings, has three parts which spiral in a way that makes them fundamentally one. The Gankyil, or 'Wheel of Joy', can clearly be seen to reflect the inseparability and interdependence of all the groups of three in the Dzogchen teachings, but perhaps most particularly it shows the inseparability of the Base, the Path, and the Fruit. And since Dzogchen, the Great Perfection, is essentially the self-perfected indivisibility of the primordial state, it naturally requires a non-dual symbol to represent it.

So the Path is not something strictly separate from the Fruit; the process of self-liberation becomes ever deeper, until the deluded consciousness that was unaware of the Base which was always our own nature disappears: this is what is called

Sewa, mixing the Fruit. The Tibetan word *sewa*, which means 'to integrate' or 'to mix', is used here because one integrates each and every

Gankyil, the Wheel of Joy

experience of ordinary life in the state of contemplation. Since in Dzogchen there is nothing to change—no special clothes to wear and nothing that may be seen from the outside—there is no way to know whether or not someone is practicing. In fact, the practice does not depend at all on outward forms; its principle is that everything in one's relative situation may be brought into the practice and integrated with the state of contemplation. This means, though, that our contemplation must of course be precise, because otherwise there would be nothing with which to integrate the experiences and actions or ordinary life. This is, if fact, implied by the second of the Three Principles of Garab Dorje, 'Not to Remain in Doubt': the practitioner no longer has any doubt as to the nature of all phenomena—which is unveiled in contemplation—because the practitioner's contemplation is perfectly precise.

Then the three capacities of Cherdrol, Shardrol, and Rangdrol are developed. The *drol* part of the name in each case means 'liberation', as in the name of the famous Bardo Thödrol, which is translated as 'liberation through hearing in the state of the

Bardo', but which is better known nowadays as 'The Tibetan Book of the Dead'.

In *Cherdrol*, the first of the three, the process of self-liberation is still at a minor capacity. Cherdrol means 'one observes and it liberates', and the example given is of the way a dewdrop evaporates when the sun shines on it.[1] But the sun in this example doesn't represent an antidote that should be applied in order to neutralize the poison of dualism. The concept of applying an antidote is alien to the spirit of the Dzogchen teachings. Rather the sun represents the manifestation of the primordial state, which naturally and automatically results in the spontaneous self-liberation of whatever arises. If, every time dualism arises as one becomes distracted from contemplation, one observes the distracting thought in order to grasp its true nature, then the obscuration of dualism self-liberates in the very moment in which the thought is clearly observed, and the primordial state is once again fully unveiled.

Shardrol is a medium capacity, and it is illustrated by the image of snow melting in the very moment that it falls into the sea.[2] Shardrol means 'as soon as it arises it liberates itself', and the snow here represents all the various kinds of sense contacts, or passions based on dualism. So as soon as there is any kind of sense contact, it liberates of itself, without even any effort being needed to maintain awareness. Even passions that would condition someone who has not reached this level of practice can simply be left as they are. This is why it is said that all one's passions, all one's karmic vision, become just like ornaments in Dzogchen, because without being conditioned by them, without being attached to them, one simply enjoys them as the play of one's own energy, which is what they are. This is why certain tantric divinities wear as an ornament a crown of five skulls which represent the five passions that have been overcome.

The most advanced capacity of self-liberation is called *Rangdrol*, which means 'of itself it liberates itself', and the example used is that of the speed and ease of a snake unwinding a knot made its own body.[3] This is completely non-dual and

Cherdrol

Shardrol

Rangdrol

all-at-once, instantaneous self-liberation. Here the illusory separation of subject and object collapses of itself, and one's habitual vision, the limited cage, the trap of ego, opens out into the spacious vision of what is. The bird is free, and can finally fly without hindrance. One can enter and enjoy the dance and play of energies, without limit.

The development of this vision is said to spread like a forest fire, until the sense of a subject subsides of its own accord. One experiences the primordial wisdom in which as soon as an object appears, one recognizes its emptiness as being the same as the voidness of one's own state. The inseparability of emptiness and vision, and the presence of the state and emptiness are all experienced together. Then everything can be said to be 'of one single taste', which is the emptiness of both subject and object. Dualism is completely overcome. Although there is, on the one hand, still the manifestation of the play of energy which, in the dualistic state, we take for objects, and, on the other hand, the cognitive capacity that in the dualistic state we take for a separate subjective self, because of the uninterrupted presence of contemplation we no longer experience the illusion of a dualism between the one and the other. This is the state pointed to in the last of the Six Vajra Verses:

Seeing that everything is self-perfected
from the very beginning,
the disease of striving for any achievement
comes to an end of its own accord,
and just remaining in the natural state as it is,
the presence of non-dual contemplation
continuously, spontaneously arises.

The interdependence of subject and object: how the senses maintain the illusion of dualism

Now, as realization deepens and increases, certain capacities may begin to manifest. But to understand these capacities at all, one must understand how the illusion of dualism is maintained by the subject-object polarity that manifests in sensory perception, which Buddhist teachings analyze in terms of six sense subjects (six sensory capacities) and six types of sensory objects. This means that, for example, that the sense of sight arises interdependently, or co-emergently, with the perception of visual form as an object. This analysis may be applied to each of the senses, until the last of the six, which is considered to be the interdependent arising of mind and existence, the interdependent arising of mind and what one experiences as one's reality.

Through an understanding of this interdependent arising of each sense and its respective object, one can understand how the illusion of duality is self-maintaining, subject implicitly implying object, and object implicitly implying subject, in the case of each sense, until finally, all the senses, including the mind, together create the illusion of an external world separate from a perceiving subject.[4] But the best way to understand this is by observing oneself: observing one's own mind, in practice, and seeing for oneself how thoughts arise like waves, and how one's senses function in relation to one's impression that one is a separate self. As Shakyamuni Buddha himself said:

> To enter contemplation for the time it takes
> for an ant to walk from one end of one's nose to the other,
> will bring more progress towards realization
> than a whole lifetime spent in the accumulation of good
> actions [merit].

With the advancing of the practice, all thoughts, and indeed all dualistic conceptualisations relating to the sensations of all the senses, self-liberate. The illusion of dualism dissolves, the apparent separation of a mental subject and its object disappears and, as a result of this, the five Ngönshes, five higher forms of awareness, may manifest in the practitioner. These are not to be sought for their own sake. They must arise, as the practice progresses, as a by-product of it, and they must not be taken as its goal.

The first of these is of the eyes, vision. It is called 'real knowledge of the eyes of the divinities', because we usually think of divinities as beings with a greater capacity than ours. What it means is that one develops the capacity, for example, to see things regardless of distance. One can even see things when they are behind other objects that get in the way of our normal vision.

The five Ngönshes

Then there is a similar capacity with regard to hearing—the 'real knowledge of hearing', or 'hearing with the ears of the divinities'. One is able to hear all sounds, regardless of distance, whether they are loud or soft, and so on.

The third capacity is the knowledge of the minds of others, in other words, being able to read other people's thoughts. The individual is made up of body, voice, and mind. What one sees with the eyes is basically physical form or body, while the capacity for hearing is related to the voice, energy, sound. Body and voice are more concrete than the mind, and so it is easier to gain the capacities relating to them. It is very difficult to know, or to understand, exactly what another person is thinking. But it is a capacity that can arise.

There is a rather humorous story of my master Changchub Dorje's clarity that illustrates these kinds of capacities well. As I have already said, Changchub Dorje practiced as a doctor, and when he had successfully cured a certain well-off patient who lived several days' journey away, that patient decided to send a servant with a gift to the master by way of thanks. The servant set out on horseback bearing the gift, which was a wrapped parcel tied up with string that contained within it many smaller packets of tea. The servant rode all day, but when he stopped for the night, still two days' ride away from Changchub Dorje's home, he decided that the master wouldn't miss a few of the packets of tea. So, pulling out his knife, he cut open the package and removed one third of them. Then he resealed and tied the now smaller parcel, so that it looked perfect, as if it had never been opened.

I was at Changchub Dorje's house two days later when the master, right out of the blue, suddenly asked his wife to prepare a meal for someone who, he said, would soon arrive. Everyone in Changchub Dorje's community was used to events that would seem strange elsewhere, and so, without question, the master's wife began to do as she was asked. Her husband requested that the meal be formally laid out with all the necessary plates and cutlery, but specifically insisted that no knife should be provided. All this was the more unusual because, unless an expected visitor was an especially important person of some kind, he or she would not normally eat separately from everyone else.

When the servant messenger at last arrived, I watched very carefully to see what would happen. He greeted the master with great respect, presenting the sealed parcel to him and conveying the thanks of his employer who had been cured. Changchub Dorje thanked him in return, and put the parcel aside saying he would open it later. Then he asked the messenger if he was hungry. When the latter replied that he was, the meal that had been prepared was served to him. The meal was a little more lavish than was usual for us, and included several courses, which the messenger ate with relish. When he came to the meat course, however, he noticed that there was no knife on the table with which to cut the meat. He had just begun to seek the knife from the scabbard hidden in the folds of his clothes, when the master fixed him with a fierce gaze and said quietly: 'It's no good searching for your knife in there, my friend. You left it on the boulder beside the road two nights ago when you used it to open the parcel intended for me and stole one third of the packets of tea!' You can perhaps understand from this why no one in Changchub Dorje's community either lied or tried to practice any deception.

The fourth capacity that may manifest on the path to realization is the knowledge of life and death. One can know, for example, when someone is going to die, in what way, and where they will be reborn. The principle of this is the development of the capacity to know time to the point of being able to go beyond time. One develops the capacity to know all the secondary causes relating to another person. The secondary causes that will manifest when that person dies are actually present in any given moment, and so can be read.

As an illustration of this capacity there is another story of a servant coming as a messenger to Changchub Dorje. This man was sent by his employer, who once again lived several days ride away, to ask for some medicine for his daughter who was seriously ill. Changchub Dorje, however, said that medicine would be of no use, as the daughter had died just after the messenger had set out to come to him, a fact that he could not have known except through his clarity. The messenger did not know whether to believe him or not, and returned home at once with medicine in case the girl should indeed turn out to still be alive, in which case his employer would say he had failed in his duty. But when he arrived home he found that the daughter had died at exactly the time Changchub Dorje had said.

The fifth capacity is called 'real knowledge of miracles'; and this is not just an intellectual understanding, but the actual concrete capacity to perform miracles. One has gone beyond all limits, and in that state such activity becomes natural rather than really miraculous at all. Miracles are usually thought of as actions someone might perform in relation to seemingly external objects, changing them in some way. But, as the division of reality into internal and external is an illusion, when that illusion is overcome it is possible to go beyond all usual limits, as the great yogi Milarepa did, when he sheltered from a hailstorm by actually getting inside a yak's horn that was lying on the ground, even though it's said that the yak's horn didn't get any bigger, and Milarepa didn't get any smaller. [See plate 19]. Another insight into the reality beyond our usual limits can be gained from the Buddha's statement that there are as many Buddhas in an atom as there are atoms in the universe. We just can't get at the meaning of such a statement within our usual framework of mental concepts, so we call such things miraculous; but this is how reality is, only we're not used to seeing it as it is. When someone actually develops the capacity to enter into what is, this is called 'the real knowledge of miracles'.

Total Integration of Subject and Object

So this is how the signs of the Path may develop for a practitioner, though they may not arise in any particular order. But now we come to a sixth capacity, a capacity of the Fruit, which is called Trödral, meaning 'beyond concept', or 'like the sky'. This involves the complete re-integration of subject and object, and is a particular Dzogchen method of attaining Total Realization in one lifetime, through the mastery of one's energy and the way that it manifests.

All the methods of the various paths, those of the sutras and all the levels of tantra, as well as those of Dzogchen, lead to Total Realization—the Fruit. This is the surpassing of conditioned existence in the manifestation of the primordial state, which endows the individual with a perfect understanding of the functioning of reality and all its phenomena, and a perfect Wisdom with manifold capacities[5]. But the sutras explain that, by applying their particular methods, it will take several *kalpa,* or aeons to attain realization.[6] And although the methods of the lower tantras are quicker, it will still require a very long time to accomplish the goal through them. The higher tantras and Dzogchen, on the other hand, both enable one to reach total realization in a single lifetime. The Visions of Longde and of the practice of Thödgal—the final and most secret teaching of Dzogchen—allow the practitioner to rapidly undo the knots of conditioned existence and attain the most absolute and total type of realization, which culminates in the complete dissolution of the physical body in the essence of its elements, which is light.

To accomplish this realization, *Semnyid*, which means the 'nature of the mind', also called the internal *ying*, is integrated with *Chodnyid*, which means the 'condition of existence', also called the 'external ying'. That they are both called *ying* (meaning 'space'; *dhatu* in Sanskrit) shows that from the beginning they are of the same nature. It's not that existence is cancelled out in some way. The Dzogchen teachings are based on the knowledge that the essential nature of the microcosm—the individual—and that of the macrocosm—the universe—are the same and, therefore, when one fully discovers and manifests one's own nature, one is discovering and manifesting the nature of the universe. The existence of duality is nothing but an illusion, and when this illusion is undone the primordial inseparability of the individual and the universe is fully discovered and the functions of that inseparability manifest; that is to say, through

Internal ying and external ying

the integration of the internal and the external ying, the Body of Light manifests. If the other five Ngönshes are signs of development on the Path, this is the ultimate expression of the Fruit .

The *Jalü* (in Tibetan), or Body of Light, realized through the practice of Dzogchen is different from the *Gyulü*, or Illusory Body, realized through the practices of the Higher Tantras. The Gyulü is dependent on the subtle prana of the individual, and thus, since prana is always considered to be of the relative dimension in Dzogchen, this Gyulü is not considered to be Total Realization. The Jalü, or Body of Light, itself, is a way of manifesting realization that is particular to the masters who have carried the practice of the Longde or of the Mennagde to their ultimate level, and with only very short breaks in the lineage, it has continued to be manifested right up to the present day.

The Body of Light

The master of my master Changchub Dorje achieved this level of realization. Changchub Dorje was present at the time, so I know it is not a fable. My master told me how his master Nyagla Padma Duddul called all his disciples together—both those who were farther away and those who were close at hand—and told them he wanted to transmit some teachings that he had until then not given them in full. So he transmitted these teachings, and then they practiced a Gana Puja together for more than a week. Gana Puja is an excellent way of eliminating disturbances between master and disciple and between disciple and disciple. Then, at the end of that week, Nyagla Padma Duddul announced to them that it was time for him to die, and that he intended to do so on a certain mountain nearby. His disciples implored him not to die, but he said that it was time, and that there was nothing to be done about it. So they all accompanied him up the mountain, to a place where he set up a little tent. Then he had his disciples sew the tent up completely, sealing him inside it, and he asked to be left in peace for seven days.

The disciples went down the mountain, and waited, camped at the foot of it for seven days, during which time it rained a great deal and there were many rainbows. Then they went back up and opened the tent, which was sewn up just as they had left it. All that they found inside was the master's clothes, his hair, and his fingernails and toenails. His clothes were the clothes of a lay person, and they remained there in a heap where he had been sitting, with the belt still wrapped around the middle. He had left them just like a snake sheds a skin. My master was present, and told me this story, so I know that it is true and that such realization is possible.

I know many other such stories, but there is a particularly interesting one that my uncle Togden told me. In 1952, in the area of Tibet that I come from there lived an old man who, when he was young, had been a kind of servant or assistant to a Dzogchen master for a few years, and who had thus naturally heard many teachings. But for the rest of his life he had just lived very simply, cutting mantras into stones for a living. He lived in this way for many years, and no one took much notice of him, or thought he was a practitioner. But then one day he announced that he was going to die in seven days' time, and sent a message to his son, who was a monk, saying that he wanted to leave all his possessions as an offering to the monastery where his son lived. The monastery spread the news far and wide that this man had said that he wanted to be left closed up for seven days to die, and since everyone understood the significance of this, many people came and the whole thing became a public event. There were representatives of all the various Buddhist schools, from the great monasteries and even members of the Chinese administration, who at that time were all military personnel. Thus, when they opened the room inside which the man had been locked for seven days, there were many people present. And what they saw was that the man had left no body. Only his hair and nails, the impurities of the body, were left.

My uncle, the yogi, came to see me at my father's house just after he had witnessed this event, and his eyes were full of tears as he told me about it. He said it was a terrible tragedy that none of us had known enough to recognize that this seemingly ordinary person, living so close to us, had actually been a very great practitioner, from whom we could have received teaching. But this is how it is with practitioners of Dzogchen. There is nothing to be seen on the outside.

When I visited Nepal in the spring of 1984 to give teachings and to practice at Tolu Gompa, a mountain monastery close to the Tibetan border, near Mount Everest, where Padmasambhava practiced, and at the cave of Maratika where Padmasambhava and his consort Mandarava realized the practice of long life, I had news of what became of my uncle Togden. This news came from a Tibetan who had just arrived in Kathmandu from Tibet, where he had been a government official in the region where Togden lived. It seems that my uncle continued to live in his isolated cave in retreat for many years after I left Tibet, but eventually, like many other similar yogis, he was made to come out of retreat in the period of the Cultural Revolution, when it was decreed that such persons were exploiters of the workers because they were provided with food even though they themselves didn't do any work. My uncle was more fortunate than many others and was only placed under house arrest, rather than having to face a public trial and possible serious punishment.

The man I met in Kathmandu had, among many other respon- sibilities, been responsible for the continuing custody of Togden, whom he allowed to live in a small, wooden house built on the flat roof of an ordinary town house in the provincial capital, a house which belonged to a Tibetan family who provided for my uncle's needs, so that he was able to continue his retreat as before. Later, because this official vouched for him, my uncle was allowed to go and live in the country under less strict supervision. There he was allocated an isolated house which the official regularly visited to keep an eye on him.

But, one day, when the official arrived there, he found the house closed up. When he managed to get in to it, he found Togden's body on his meditation couch; but the body had shrunk to the size of that of a small child. The official was very worried: how was he to explain such a thing to his Chinese superiors. He was afraid they would probably believe that he was aiding

Togden's escape in some way, and so he went at once to inform them of what had happened.

But when he returned to the isolated house a few days later with all the high-ranking officers of the regional government, Togden's body had disappeared completely. Only the hair and the fingernails were left. The official's Chinese superiors were completely bewildered and anxiously asked for an explanation, but the Tibetan official could only say that he had heard that ancient texts spoke about yogis realizing what was called a 'Body of Light', although he had never expected to see such a thing himself.

This event made such an impression on him that he developed a strong interest in spiritual matters, and as soon as he could, managed to escape on foot into Nepal where he felt he would be free to receive teachings and practice, and where I met him. I was deeply moved to hear of my uncle's realization. Knowing how serious a problem he had had with various mental disturbances in his early life, I did not expect him to achieve so much in one lifetime. His example shows what is possible for every individual.

To use the metaphor of the mirror once again, the realization of the Body of Light means that one is no longer in the condition of a person who is reflected in a mirror and who dualistically sees his or her own reflection in it, but one has become established in the essential condition of the mirror so that one's energy as a whole now manifests in the same way that the energy of a mirror does. Knowing how one's own energy manifests as Dang, Rolpa, and Tsal, one is able to integrate one's energy completely right through to the level of actual material existence. This is accomplished either through the visions of the Longde that arise as a result of the practices of the four *Da*, or through the practice of the Four Lights that bring about the arising of the Four Visions of Thödgal, which develop in very much the same way as the visions of the Longde develop.

The Way of Light

The first of these Four Visions of Thödgal is called the 'Vision of Dharmata' (or 'nature of reality'), and the second vision is the further development of the first. The third is the maturation of it, and the fourth is the consummation of existence. If, while alive, one has entered the third level of these visions, and to say one has 'entered' means that there are certain signs that this is so, then, when one dies, one's body slowly disappears into light. Instead of decomposing into its constituent elements in the usual way, it dissolves into the essence of its elements, which is light. The process may take longer than seven days to happen. All that remains of the physical body are the hair and fingernails, which are considered to be its impurities. The rest of the body has dissolved into the essence of its elements. This is the realization that garab Dorje, and, more recently, many other masters, a few of whom I have mentioned as examples, achieved.

A practitioner who manifests this realization cannot really be said to have 'died', at all, in the ordinary sense of the word because he or she still remains spontaneously active as a principle of being in a Body of Light. The spontaneous activity of such an individual will be directed for the benefit of others, and he or she is actually visible to someone in a physical body who has sufficient clarity.

But a practitioner who perfects and completes the fourth level of the Thödgal visions does not manifest death at all, but while still living gradually becomes invisible to those who have normal karmic vision. This level of realization is called the 'Great Transfer', and this is the realization that Padmasambhava and Vimalamitra manifested. Essentially, the realizations of the Great Transfer and the Body of Light are one and the same; the only difference is that those who attain the Great Transfer do not have to go through death in the clinical sense in order to move

The Great Transfer

from manifestation in the material plane to manifestation in the plane of the essence of elements. These two modes of realization are particular to the practice of Dzogchen

Total Realization

Ordinary beings are reborn without choice, conditioned by their karma into taking a body according to the causes they have accumulated over countless past lives. A totally realized being, on the other hand, is free from the cycle of conditioned cause and effect. But such a being may manifest a body through which others can have the possibility of being helped. The Body of Light, or the Light Body of a being who has realized the Great Transfer, are both phenomena which can be actively maintained so that those having the visionary clarity necessary for perceiving them can communicate with the fully realized individuals whose bodies find themselves in a dimension of pure light.

The three bodies: Nirmanakaya, Sambhoga- kaya, Dharmakaya

But to help those who lack such capacity, a totally realized being may manifest in an actual physical body in the way that, for example, garab Dorje and the Buddha did. All these kinds of bodies are of the Nirmanakaya; *kaya* in Sanskrit, means 'body', or 'dimension', and *nirmana* means manifestation. So a totally realized individual may choose to manifest a Body of Light, or voluntarily take a rebirth in an ordinary physical body in the gross material dimension, but is not conditioned by such a body, or by the actions carried out in it.

The Sambhogakaya, or 'Body of Wealth', is the dimension of the essence of the elements that make up the gross material world, a subtle dimension of light appearing in a wealth of forms which can only be perceived through the development of clarity of awareness and visionary capacity. A totally realized being may manifest a Sambhogakaya form, but in such a form is not active as is a being who manifests in a Body of Light.

Just as the rays of the sun are a manifestation of its inherent qualities, so too the wisdom of a totally realized individual is what that individual is. Each Sambhogakaya form is a personification of a principle of pure wisdom. But just as the sun does not intend to send its rays to any particular place, and it depends on the characteristics of the place as to whether it will receive the rays, it is the practitioner who must be active to perceive the dimension of the Sambhogakaya and gain access to the wisdom personified by a particular Sambhogakaya form, opening that dimension in him or herself.

Although the capacity to manifest either Sambhogakaya or Nirmanakaya forms is a facet of Total Realization, such realization means that one has gone beyond all limits and all forms. One has made manifest that state which always is, and was one's true condition from the beginning, although, in samsara, it has been hidden from deluded mind by the experience of the illusion of dualism. Total realization means that one has realized one's identity with the Dharmakaya, the 'Body of Truth', or 'Dimension of Reality as it is'. It is the omnipresent void matrix, the Zhi, or Base of every individual that manifests in the infinitely interpenetrating dance of the energies of the universe as the Sambhogakaya and Nirmanakaya forms of a realized individual; or as the limited cage of karmic vision—the body, voice, and mind—of a being trapped in dualism who mistakes his or her own energy for a seemingly separate external world.

Total Realization means the definitive end of illusion, the end of suffering, the cessation of the vicious cycle of conditioned rebirths; it is the dawning of complete freedom, perfect wisdom, supreme unending bliss. In Total Realization death is overthrown, all duality transcended, and the capacity to spontaneously benefit all beings is perfectly manifested in a multiplicity of modes. Of all the possible rebirths in any of the Six Realms, birth in a human body is the most favorable for working towards Total Realization; and to be truly human, to fulfil truly one's humanity, such realization must be one's goal. Otherwise, one lives one's life, as the Buddha pointed out, like a preoccupied child playing with toys in a house that is burning to the ground.

For an ordinary human being death is real, and may come at any time, without warning. To waste one's precious human rebirth in trivial concerns is a tragedy. Only practice leads to one's own realization, and only through one's own realization can one ultimately help others, manifesting the capacities to be able to guide them to attain that same state themselves; any material assistance one can offer can only ever be provisional. To be able to help others one must therefore begin by helping oneself, however contradictory that may sound. Just as in counting to a million one must begin counting at the number one, so to benefit society, one must begin by working on oneself. Each individual must truly take responsibility for him or herself, and this can only be done by working to increase one's awareness, to become more fully conscious, more the master of oneself.

Change on a small scale can bring about change on a wider scale; the influence of one being who is progressing towards realization can be powerful both at the level of subtle spiritual influence and in the concrete terms of influencing society. My own master Changchub Dorje, for example, was not a person who was considered to be a master because he had been officially recognized as a reincarnation. He was an ordinary person who had followed several great Dzogchen masters, and who had put what they had taught him into practice. But through the power of his practice he manifested great clarity, and as a result of his qualities he came to be regarded as a master, and disciples then began to come to find him. He didn't live in a monastery, but in an ordinary house, as I have already remarked in some of the stories I have told about him, and his disciples, who included both monks and lay people, as they arrived, gradually built more houses as the years went by, until a village of practitioners had grown up around him. The kind of village that developed is known as a *gar*, a term which has the sense of being the temporary or seasonal residence of nomads who may move on at any time—perhaps, for example, when all the grass in an area has been grazed.

With the passing of time, all kinds of people, young and old, rich and poor, lay and ordained, came to live together in Changchub Dorje's gar. There was a daily provision of free soup and simple fare for those who had no resources of their own, and this was paid for by those who had more than sufficient for their needs. Inspired by the master everyone offered what contributions they could to the needs of the whole community. Those practitioners who lacked private means were thus enabled to live, receive teachings, and practice at the gar; but everyone who lived there worked every day participating in the hard physical labor of cultivating the fields, as well as collecting herbs and preparing medicines. In this way, as the influence of the master spread through this group of individuals drawn from all walks of life and all social strata, and as each individual's awareness developed, a kind of cooperative that was unknown at that time in Tibet spontaneously arose. The master never decreed that this was the way things should be; he encouraged the development of the awareness of his disciples, and out of their awareness this response to their practical situation and everyday needs evolved. The pattern of the gar was quite different from the feudal system that still generally prevailed in Tibet.

When Changchub Dorje arrived in the region where his gar gradually grew up around him, he was already an old man. People would ask him how old he was, and he would always reply that he was seventy. He was still saying that he was seventy when I met him in 1955—sixty years after his arrival in that region. I myself, out of curiosity, asked him several times how old he was, and he always told me that he was seventy. But the people of the area reckoned that he must at that time have been at least one hundred and thirty years old.

We walk, we work, we eat, and we sleep, and all of these activities must be permeated with our practice so that none of our time is wasted in our progress towards realization. Although Changchub Dorje was continually active for the benefit of others, and worked every day at his practice of medicine, his own progress towards realization was in no way impaired. Despite his ordinary lifestyle he was a thoroughly extraordinary man. He died at a remarkably old age, having brought his life's work to conclusion, leaving an invaluable legacy both in the teachings he gave that were written down and in the hearts and minds of his students.

As a result of my coming to live in the West I have travelled all over the world in response to requests that I teach Dzogchen, and wherever I go it is always my hope that the inspiration of the life and teachings of Changchub Dorje will be a cause of awakening for all those who hear of them. May it be auspicious!

This concludes the presentation here of the Base, the Path, and the Fruit of the Dzogchen teachings. While words and intellectual concepts can only ever be signposts pointing to the true nature of reality, which is quite beyond them, nevertheless the complex interlinked conceptual structure of the teachings is in itself brilliant and beautiful, like a many-faceted crystal whose every facet flawlessly reflects and refers to every other. But please remember that the only way to look into the heart of that crystal is to look into oneself. Dzogchen is not just something to be studied; the Way of Light is there to be travelled.

> As a bee seeks nectar
> from all kinds of flowers,
> seek teachings everywhere.
>
> Like a deer that finds a quiet place to graze,
> seek seclusion to digest all you have gathered.
>
> Like a lion, live completely free of all fear.
> And, finally, like a madman, beyond all limits,
> go wherever you please.

—*A Tantra of Dzogchen*

Appendix One

A. Garab Dorje's Three Principles of the Dzogchen Teaching

(1) *Direct Introduction*: the primordial state is transmitted straight away by the master to the disciple. The master always remains in the primordial state, and the presence of the state is thus communicated to the disciple in whatever situation or activity they may share.

(2) *Not To Remain in Doubt*: through the repeated experience of the primordial state in contemplation, the disciple no longer has any doubts about what his or her true condition is.

(3) *To Continue In the State*: the disciple endeavors to continue at all times in the state of non-dual contemplation, the primordial state, until every thought or experience spontaneously self-liberates in the very instant that it arises, without any effort being necessary, and nothing any longer hides the true condition of the individual (which is obscured, in *samsara*, by dualistic vision). One continues right up to Total Realization (p.162).

B. Key to the Groups of Three in the Dzogchen teachings

A linear diagram cannot truly represent the complex inter-relationships of the various aspects of the teachings, which would be better represented by a three-dimensional crystalline structure, each of whose points connected with every other. But, since a book is a linear presentation because of the very nature of language and how it is written, the teaching, when written in a book, has to be presented in a linear sequence. So this diagram is only intended as a provisional key to be of use towards opening up a more subtle vision of the many correspondences in the crystal of the teachings, and as an aid to following the argument of the book.

1. BASE The primordial state,
   or base of every individual
   which comprises:

> — ESSENCE, which is void
> — NATURE, yet manifestation continues to occur
> — ENERGY, which manifests in three characteristic ways as:
>
>> — DANG   These, as is explained by the examples of
>> — ROLPA   the crystal and its rays, the crystal ball,
>> — TSAL   and the mirror and its reflections, are
>>   one's own energy. Yet a being in Samsara
>>   mistakes them for external phenomena,
>>   and sees them as his karmic vision,
>>   comprising respectively:
>>
>>> — MIND
>>> — VOICE (or energy con-
>>>   nected to breathing)
>>> — BODY

2. PATH

— TAWA, View, or Vision of the true condition of the individual
   and of the universe. The true view is to observe the condition of
   one's own true mind, voice, and body.

— GOMPA, Actual practices presented in the Three Series. There are
   practices that work with each of the aspects of the individual
   Body, Voice, and Mind.

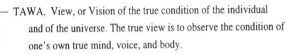

— SEMDE, the Series of Mind
— LONGDE, the Series of Space
— MENNAGDE, the Essential Series

PRINCIPAL PRACTICES are the practice of contemplation, of Dzogchen itself, and meditation practices leading one to be able to enter contemplation.
The practices of TREGCHÖD help one to be able to
recognize the primordial state and to continue in contemplation, while the practices of THÖDGAL rapidly
enable one to develop the state of contemplation,
through vision, to its ultimate conclusion, in the realization of the Body of Light.

SECONDARY PRACTICES are any practice that
may be used together with contemplation, to develop
a particular capacity, or to overcome a particular
obstacle, such as Yantra Yoga, recitation of mantras,
ritual, and so on.

— CHÖDPA, conduct in daily life: how one lives in the light of the Tawa,
   or View, and the practice, maintaining non-dual contemplation in
   every action of the 24 hours of one's daily life, or if one cannot
   succeed in that, at least maintaining the presence of self-observing
   awareness.

3. FRUIT or, Realization.

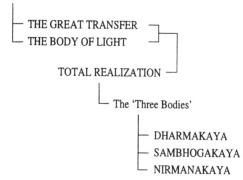

├─ THE GREAT TRANSFER
└─ THE BODY OF LIGHT

      TOTAL REALIZATION

            └─ The 'Three Bodies'

                ├─ DHARMAKAYA
                ├─ SAMBHOGAKAYA
                └─ NIRMANAKAYA

The Three Bodies are the correct perception of the three ways of manifestation of energy (Dang, Rolpa and Tsal) and of the three aspects of the Base that they illustrate—which have always been the true condition of each and every individual and of the whole universe.

C. Summary of the methods of the various paths of Sutra, Tantra and Dzogchen according to the Nyingmapa tradition

The three schools of Tibetan Buddhism that arose after the Nyingmapa—the Sakyapa, the Kagyüdpa, and the Gelugpa schools—classify the tantras in a different way from the manner in which they are classified in the Nyingmapa school, speaking for example, of 'Higher' (Anuttara) and 'Lower' tantras, rather than of 'Inner' and 'Outer' tantras. But since the purpose of this brief summary is to give the reader a key to understanding the relationship between Dzogchen and the various levels of tantra, we will concentrate here on the classification found within the Nyingmapa school—the school most closely associated with Dzogchen.

The term *Dzogchen* itself needs some further explanation at this point, since it can be used in two senses, either:

(i) to indicate the whole of the 'Path of Self-Liberation', with its three aspects, Base, Path, and Fruit, or:

(ii) to refer to the Fruit, or realization, of the Anuyoga (one of the tantric vehicles found in the Nyingmapa school, that will be considered below).

The same name *Dzogchen* is used in both instances because the same state, the state of Dzogchen, is both the starting point of the Path of Self-Liberation (introduced right away in the Direct Introduction given by the Master to the disciple) and the Fruit (or realization) of the Anuyoga.

When we speak of Dzogchen in its first sense, as the Path of Self-Liberation, it belongs to neither sutra nor tantra, is not a gradual Path, and does not see itself as the high point of a hierarchy of levels.

Nor is Dzogchen, in the sense of the Path of Self-Liberation, part of the tantric Path of Transformation (see below): it does not use visualization as a principal practice, although, being beyond all limits, it may use methods of any level of tantra as secondary practices.

The main practice in Dzogchen consists in entering directly into non-dual contemplation and remaining in that state, constantly making it deeper until Total Realization is attained.

The various levels of Tantra—i.e., of the Vajrayana—have as their foundation and starting point the emptiness of all phenomena, the principle of shunyata. All of them function on the basis of this principle through the application of visualization, but the practice of visualization is applied differently in each level in order to reintegrate the individual's energy with the energy of the universe from which it appears to have become separate.

Whereas the Sarmapa or 'new' schools (the Sakyapa, Kagyüdpa, and Gelugpa) consider Anuttaratantra ('supreme tantra'); or Anuttarayogatantra to be the supreme vehicle, the Nyingmapa speak of three Inner Tantras (Atiyoga, Anuyoga, and Mahayoga, of which Atiyoga and AnuYoga are only found in the Nyingmapa school).

Atiyoga is the Path of Self-Liberation, and it does not involve visualization. Through the Direct Introduction given by the master one recognizes the primordial state of mind, the mind's natural condition, the state of Dzogchen, and then, by means of various practices, one deepens one's capacity to know that state, until one can remain in it at all times, integrating all one's actions with non-dual contemplation.

Although Atiyoga as such does not belong to the Path of Transformation of Tantra, its root texts are nevertheless called tantras and, ever since the second spread of the teachings in Tibet, it has been included among the Inner Tantras and considered to be the supreme level of Tantra. In the same way, although Atiyoga is not a gradual path—for in it one begins immediately with Direct Introduction to the state of Dzogchen—it may also be approached by those who have been 'climbing' through the successive stages of the gradual path, as the latter's last stage. So in a presentation of the gradual path it would appear as its supreme and final stage. Atiyoga is only found in the Nyingmapa school.

Anuyoga is a method of the Path of Transformation. The aim of the Path of Transformation in general is to enable the practitioner to transform impure vision into pure vision, which is done by means of visualizing a divinity and his or her mandala, thus entering the pure dimension of the divinity.

Anuyoga is only found in Nyingmapa school, and it uses a form of visualization not found elsewhere: the visualization is manifested in an instant rather than it being built up gradually detail by detail as in the other yogas.

At the Anuyoga level, one visualizes oneself as the deity, rather than visualizing the divinity as external to oneself, and the powerful sensation of being the 'deity' oneself is considered more important than the formation of a complete mental image of all the various details of the divinity and his or her surrounding mandala.

Mahayoga is also a practice of the Path of Transformation. As in the Anuyoga, one visualizes oneself as the 'deity', but here the visualization of the 'divinity' and mandala is built up gradually, detail by detail. The Fruit of the Mahayoga is called 'Mahamudra' ('Total Symbol')[4].

Yogatantra is the first level of the Path of Transformation. Here, too, one visualizes oneself as the 'deity', and begins the work with the internal yoga using the subtle energy of the body that continues in the levels of the Path of Transformation above.

In *Upayatantra,* 'deity' or realized individual who is used as the basis of practice is here first visualized as being external to oneself, though as one's equal rather than as essentially superior to oneself, and one works with some inner yoga, as well as with external actions.

Kriyatantra is the level of the Path of Purification properly speaking, and here one visualizes the deity as external to oneself, and superior to oneself. One works with external actions only, to purify oneself to be able to receive wisdom from the realized being, purifying one's entire dimension with the aim of realizing the pure state of the 'divinity', which is in fact one's own condition from the beginning.

In *Sutra*, the Path of Renunciation, the emphasis is on giving up, or renouncing, negative actions and adopting positive actions, while Tantra seeks to purify or transform the negative tendencies of body, voice and mind into positive ones.

Both the Hinayana (which includes both the Shravakayana and the Pratyekabuddhayana) and Mahayana levels of the Sutra path work towards the experience of Shunyata, or voidness—which is Tantra's starting point. Tantra assumes that all phenomena are without inherent self-nature, and works on that assumption to work with the play of energy that makes up the world of appearances.

Gradual paths insist that a practitioner must work from here upwards. Dzogchen, on the other hand, doesn't adopt a hierarchical approach; it proceeds right away on the basis of the master giving the student a Direct Introduction to the primordial state to enable the student to recognize that state for him or herself, and then to remain in it.

Dzogchen is beyond limits, and practices of any of the other levels can be used as secondary practices by a Dzogchen practitioner. But the principal practice of Dzogchen is to enter directly into non-dual contemplation, and to remain in it, continuing to deepen it until one reaches Total Realization.

D. Principal Practices of the Three Series of the Dzogchen Teachings

Semde: the Series of the Nature of Mind

Four Naljor, or Yogas: to enable one to enter contemplation

1. Shiné: 'calm state'

   Through fixation with an object, and without an object, one arrives at a state of calm. This becomes natural, then stable.

2. Lhagthong: 'more vision', or insight

   The state of calm is dissolved, or 'awakened'. One is able to practice with the movement of thought without the effort of maintaining an internal 'watcher'; the state of calm is no longer something constructed.

3. Nyimed: 'non-duality'

   Shiné and Lhagthong arise together; one goes beyond duality.

4. Lhundrub: 'self-perfection'

   Non-dual contemplation can be carried into every action. All is totally reintegrated in its own natural condition, and one experiences everything that arises as the self-perfected play of one's own energy. This is the practice of Dzogchen, the Great Perfection.

Longde: the Series of Space

Four Da, or Symbols: to enable one to enter contemplation

1. Salwa: 'clarity'

   The eyes are open; the whole of the individual's vision is integrated. This is not the same as intellectual clarity.

2. Mitogpa: 'non-conceptuality'

   With open eyes fixed in empty space, unblinking, whatever thought arises, it does not disturb.

3. Dewa: 'blissful sensation'

   The body is kept in a controlled position until one is more developed in the practice, yet it is almost as if the body were not there—although one is completely present. Lightly clenching the muscles of the 'lower gates' of the body increases the naturally blissful sensation of complete relaxation.

4. Yermed: 'inseparability' (sometimes translated imprecisely as 'union')
    The inseparability of all the other three Da in the state of contemplation
    and the practice of Dzogchen. As a symbol of this inseparability, one
    keeps the tongue loose, touching neither the roof nor the floor of the
    mouth.
All the four Da are practiced simultaneously, together.

Mennagde: The Essential Series

Four Chogshag (literally, 'as it is'): although this series also has practices
to enable one to enter into contemplation—such as the Internal and External
Rushen and the 21 Semdzin—the four Chogshag, which enable the practitioner to continue in contemplation, are what is essential to it.

1. Riwo Chogshag: Chogshag of the Mountain
    This refers to the body. The body is left 'as it is'. Whatever the position
    of the body, that is the position of practice.
2. Gyamtso Chogshag: Chogshag of the Ocean
    Refers to the eyes. No particular gaze is needed. Whatever the position of
    the eyes, that is the position of practice.

3. Rigpa Chogshag: Chogshag of the state of contemplation
    One's own state is left as it is, without correction. This Chogshag is the
    same as Lhundrub in the Semde, and Yermed in the Longde.

4. Nangwa Chogshag: Chogshag of vision
    All of one's vision is said to be 'as an ornament'. One experiences all
    one's karmic vision as one's own energy, whether as Dang, Rolpa or
    Tsal.

The four Chogshag manifest simultaneously in the same instant, and this is
    Dzogchen. The state of contemplation arrived at is the same in each of
    the Three Series.

Alternative terminology for three aspects of the practice of the Semde

The terms 'Shiné', 'Lhagtong', and 'Nyimed' belong more properly to the
Sutra and Tantra levels of the teachings, but because they are more generally
known and used, we have used them here. The terms that are usually found in
Dzogchen texts for the same phases of practice are:
    (1) Nepa (calm state; literally, 'the space between one thought and the
next') in Dzogchen, one has already received Direct Introduction to the
Primordial State from the master when one begins to practice the Semde, so,

this first contemplation of the Semde is not exactly the same as the practice of Shiné in the Sutra system, because experience of the state of pure presence, or rigpa, is involved from the beginning in Dzogchen. Thus, if one were to speak of the four Naljor of the Semde as being 'gradual'—in the sense that one applies the Naljor one by one—one would have to qualify that statement by saying that the Semde could also be called 'non-gradual' because in Dzogchen one is always introduced to one's own state right from the beginning. In fact it might be better to say that Dzogchen is neither gradual nor non-gradual: in the Semde one is introduced by the master to the primordial state right away, but one then develops and deepens the state of contemplation gradually through the four Naljor. When the master introduces the state, we usually recognize it, but we may have doubts that make it hard for us to remain in it. So the development of the calm state of Nepa is very important to develop the practitioner's confidence, so that he or she 'does not remain in doubt' about his or her true condition—the second of Garab Dorje's Three Principles.

(2) Migyurwa ('non-movement') This stage of the practice of the Semde is concerned with the development of 'clarity'. One has found the state of rigpa (or pure presence) through the calm state (Nepa) of the first Naljor, and now, from the point of view of this pure presence, the movement of thought becomes just the same as if it were non-movement. The usual experience of sentient beings is for thought to continually arise without interruption, and for them to be conditioned into dualism by that thought. In fact thoughts arise with such intensity for many people that they don't even notice that there is a space between one thought and another. But when one has the capacity to remain in a state of pure presence as in the Migyurwa Naljor of the Semde, thought can arise but it no longer has any power to disturb. So, whereas thought is considered to be an obstacle to meditation in the Shiné of the Sutra system, wherein one seeks shelter from the storm of thought (as it were) in the state of calm, it is said that for a Dzogchen practitioner 'the more thoughts there are, the more wisdom', because (in this case at this stage in the development of the practitioner of the Semde) one is able to integrate one's thoughts in contemplation, and the arising of thought then actually strengthens the clarity of the state of rigpa rather than distracting the practitioner.

(3) Nyamnyid (equanimity, the state in which all is of the same taste, i.e., non-dual) This is the real starting point of contemplation in the Semde. One has the capacity to integrate the objects of the senses. All sense objects are now experienced as the energy of the Primordial State.

(4) Lhundrub ('self-perfected', as in the other system of terminology for the stages of the practice of the Semde). At this point the practitioner no

longer needs to apply effort. This is the stage of Enlightenment. One continues and deepens the capacity of integration, integrating first the functions of the mind, then of the energy and, finally, of the body. The realization of the Body of Light is the ultimate integration of the body.

It is also worth noting that the term 'Naljor', for which 'yoga' or 'union' is generally given as the Sanskrit equivalent, could be taken to imply a union of two things, whereas in fact, no notion of two things that need to be united exists in the non-dual View of Dzogchen. 'Naljor' is formed from the noun *nalma*, which means 'the natural, unaltered state (of something)', and the verb *jorwa*, which means 'to possess', so that the two parts of the term taken together aptly expressed the concept of the 'discovery of the natural, or primordial, state'.

Again, for the same reason that there is no notion of a need to unify a duality in Dzogchen, the four phases of practice in the Semde, rather than being referred to as the Four Yogas, are commonly called 'the four *Tingedzin*', or concentrations.

Appendix Two

Biographical sketch of the author

This short biography was originally published in the second edition in Tibetan of the author's Necklace of Gzi: A Cultural History of Tibet, *published by the Private Office of H.H. The Dalai Lama. It was translated into English by John Reynolds to be included in Chögyal Namkhai Norbu's booklet* Dzogchen and Zen, *published by Zhang Zhung Editions, Oakland, California, 1984. It is included here as a more complete biography than Rinpoche's anecdotal account of his early life in the first chapter of this book. Since this biography will be of interest primarily to Tibetologists, we have left the Tibetan names and terms in the transcription system in which the material was originally published.*

Nam mkha'i Norbu Rinpoche was born in the village of dGe'ug, in the lCong ra district of sDe dge in East Tibet on the seventh, eighth, or ninth day of the tenth month of the Earth Tiger year (1938) (the exact day is uncertain in his family's collective memory). His father was sGrol ma Tshe ring, member of a noble family and sometime official with the government of sDe dge, and his mother was Ye shes Chos sgron.

When he was two years old, dPal yul Karma Yang srid Rinpoche[1] and Zhe chen Rab byams Rinpoche,[2] both recognized him as the reincarnation of A 'dzom 'Brug pa. A 'dzom 'Brug pa was one of the great rDzogs chen Masters of the early part of this century. He was the disciple of the first mKhyen brtse Rinpoche, 'Jam dbyangs mKhyen brtse dBang po (1829-92), and also the disciple of dPal sprul Rinpoche.[4] Both of these illustrious teachers were leaders of the *Ris med* or non-sectarian movement in nineteenth-century eastern Tibet. On some thirty-seven occasions, A 'dzom 'Brug pa received transmissions from his principal master, 'Jam dbyangs mKhyen brtse, and from dPal sprul Rinpoche he received the complete transmissions of the *kLong chen snying thig* and the *rTsa rlung* precepts. In turn, A 'dzom 'Brug pa became a *gter ston*, or discoverer of hidden treasure texts, having received visions directly from the incomparable 'Jigs med gLing pa (1730-98) at the age of thirty. Teaching at A 'dzom sgar in eastern Tibet during summer and winter retreats,[5] A 'dzom 'Brug pa became the master of many contemporary teachers of rDzogs chen. Among them was Norbu Rinpoche's paternal uncle, rTogs ldan Orgyan bsTan 'dzin,[6] who was his first rDzogs chen teacher.

When he was eight years old, the sixteenth Karmapa,[7] and dPal spung Situ Rinpoche[8] both recognized Norbu Rinpoche to be the mind-incarnation[9] of Lho 'Brug Zhabs drung Rinpoche.[10] This latter master, the reincarnation of the illustrious 'Brug pa bKa' brgyud master Padma dKar po (1527-92), was the actual historical founder of the state of Bhutan. Until the early twentieth century, the Zhabs drung Rinpoches were the Dharmarajas or temporal and spiritual rulers of Bhutan.

While yet a child, from rDzogs chen mKhan Rinpoche,[11] from his maternal uncle mKhyen brtse Yang srid Rinpoche,[12] and from his paternal uncle rTogs ldan Orgyan bsTan 'dzin, Norbu Rinpoche received instruction in the *rDzogs chen gsang ba snying thig* and the *sNying thig Ya bzhi*. Meanwhile, from gNas rgyab mChog sprul Rinpoche,[13] he received the transmissions of the *rNying ma bka' ma*, the *kLong gsal rdo rje snying po*, and the *gNam chos* of Mi 'gyur rDo rje. From mKhan Rinpoche dPal ldan Tshul khrims (1906-) he received the transmissions from the *rGyud sde kun btus*, the famous Sa skya pa collection of tantric practices. And, in addition, he received many initiations and listened to many oral explanations[14] from the famous Ris rmed pa, or nonsectarian masters, of eastern Tibet.

From the time he was eight years old until he was twelve, he attended the college of sDe dge dbon stod slob grwa at sDe dge dgon chen Monastery, where, with mKhen Rinpoche mKhyen rab Chos kyi 'od zer (1901-), he studied the thirteen basic texts[15] used in the standard academic curriculum designed by mKhan po gZhan dga'.[16] Norbu Rinpoche became especially expert in the *Abhisamayālaṅkāra*. In addition, with this same master he studied the great commentary to the *Kālacakra* tantra,[17] the *Guhyagarbha* tantra, the *Zab mo nang don* of Karmapa Rang byung rDo rje, the Medical tantras,[18] Indian and Chinese astrology,[19] as well as receiving from him the initiations and transmissions of the *Sa skya'i sgrub thabs kun btus*. From the age of eight until he was fourteen, at the college of sDe dge Ku se gSer ljongs bshad grwa, from mKhan Rinpoche Brag gyab Blos gros (1913-), he received instructions in the Prajñāpāramitā sūtras, the *Abhisamayālaṅkāra*, and three tantric texts: the *rDo rje Gur*, the *Hevajra* tantra and the *Samputa* tantra.[20] By his tutor mChog sprul Rinpoche[21] he was instructed in the secular sciences.[22]

Also, from the age of eight until he was fourteen, having gone to rDzong gsar Monastery in eastern Tibet, he received teachings from the illustrious rDzong gsar mKhyen brtse Rinpoche[23] on the *Sa skya'i zab chos lam 'bras*, the quintessential doctrine of the Sa skya pa school, and in addition, on the three texts: *rGyud kyi spyi don rnam bzhag, lJon shing chen mo*, and the *Hevajra* tantra.[24] Then at the college of Khams bre bshad grwa, with mKhan Rinpoche Mi nyag Dam chos (1920-) he studied a basic text on logic, the *Tshad ma rig gter* of Sa skya Paṇḍita.

Then, in the meditation cave at Seng-chen gNam brag, he made a retreat with his uncle the rTogs ldan O rgyan bsTan 'dzin for the practices of Vajrapāṇi, Siṃhamukha, and White Tārā. At that time, the son of A 'dzom 'Brug pa,'Gyur med rDo rje (1895-), returned from Central Tibet, and, staying with them, the latter bestowed the cycle of rDo rje gro lod, the Klong chen snying thig, and the cycle of the dGongs pa zang thal of Rig 'dzin rGod ldem 'Phru can.

When he was fourteen years old in 1951, he received the initiations for Vajrayogini according to the Ngor pa and Tshar pa traditions of the Sa skya. Then his tutor advised him to seek out a woman living in the Kadari region who was the living embodiment of Vajrayogini herself and take initiation from her. This woman master, A yo mKha' 'gro rDo rje dPal sgron (1838-1953), was a direct disciple of the great 'Jam dbyangs mKhyen brtse dBang po and of Nyag bla Padma bDud 'dul, as well as being an elder contemporary of A 'dzom 'Brug pa. At this time she was 113 years old and had been in a dark retreat[25] for some fifty-six years. Norbu Rinpoche received from her transmissions for the *mKha' 'gro gsang 'dus*, the mind-treasure[26] of 'Jam dbyangs mKhyen brtse dBang po, and the *mKha' 'gro yang thig*, in which the principal practice is the dark retreat, as well as the *kLong chen snying thig*. She also bestowed upon him her own mind-treasures, including that for the Ḍākinī Siṃhamukha, the *mKha' 'gro dbang mo'i seng ge gdong ma'i zab thig*.

Then in 1954, he was invited to visit the People's Republic of China as a representative of Tibetan youth. From 1954 he was an instructor in Tibetan language at the Southwestern University of Minor Nationalities at Chengdu, Sichuan, China. While living in China, he met the famous Gangs dkar Rinpoche.[27] From the master he heard many explanations of the Six Doctrines of Nāropa,[28] Mahāmudrā, the *dKon mchog spyi 'dus*, as well as Tibetan medicine. During this time, Norbu Rinpoche also acquired proficiency in the Chinese and Mongolian languages.

When he was seventeen years old, returning to his home country of sDe dge following a vision received in dream, he came to meet his Root Master,[29] Nyag bla Rinpoche Rig 'dzin Byang chub rDo rje (1826-1978), who lived in a remote valley to the east of sDe dge. Byang chub rDo rje Rinpoche hailed originally from the Nyag rong region on the borders of China. He was a disciple of A 'dzom 'Brug pa, of Nyag bla Padma dDud 'dul, and of Shar rdza Rinpoche,[30] the famous Bönpo teacher of rDzogs chen who attained the Rainbow Body of Light.[31] A practicing physician, Byang chub rDo rje Rinpoche headed a commune called Nyag bla sGar in this remote valley; it was a totally self-supporting community consisting entirely of lay practitioners, yogins, and yoginis. From this master, Norbu Rinpoche received initiation into, and transmission of, the essential teachings of rDzogs chen *Sems sde, Klong sde,* and *Man ngag gi sde.* More importantly, this master introduced him directly to the experience of rDzogs chen. He remained here for almost a year, often assisting Byang chub rDo rje Rinpoche in his medical practice and serving as his scribe and secretary. He also received transmissions from the master's son, Nyag sras 'Gyur med rDo rje. After this, Norbu Rinpoche set out on a prolonged pilgrimage to Central Tibet, Nepal, India, and Bhutan. Returning to sDe dge, the land of his birth, he found that deteriorating political conditions had led to the eruption of violence. Fleeing first toward Central Tibet, he finally emerged safely in Sikkim as a refugee. From 1958 to 1960 he lived in Gangtok, Sikkim, employed as an author and editor of Tibetan textbooks for the Development Office, the Government of Sikkim. In 1960 when he was twenty-two years old, at the invitation of Professor Giuseppe Tucci, he went to Italy and resided for several years in Rome. During this time, from 1960 to 1964, he was a research associate at the Istituto Italiano per il Medio ed Estremo Oriente. Receiving a grant from the Rockefeller Foundation, he worked in close collaboration with Professor Tucci, and wrote two appendices to Professor Tucci's *Tibetan Folk Songs of Gyantse and Western Tibet* (Rome, 1966), as well as giving seminars at IsMEO on yoga, medicine, and astrology.

From 1964 to 1994, Norbu Rinpoche was a professor at the Istituto Orientale, University of Naples, where he taught Tibetan language, Mongolian language, and Tibetan cultural history. Since then he has done extensive research into the historical origins of Tibetan culture, investigating little-known literary sources from the Bönpo tradition. In 1983, Norbu Rinpoche hosted the first International Convention on Tibetan Medicine held at Venice, Italy. While still actively teaching at the university and since his retirement from his post as professor there, Norbu Rinpoche has informally conducted teaching retreats in various countries, including Italy, France, England, Austria, Denmark, Norway, Finland, and since 1979, the United States. During these retreats, he gives practical instruction in rDzogs chen practices in a non-sectarian format, as well as teaching aspects of Tibetan culture, especially Yantra Yoga, Tibetan medicine and astrology. Moreover, under his guidance there has grown up, at first in Italy and now in several other countries, including the United States, what has come to be known as the Dzogchen Community.[32] This is an informal association of individuals who, while continuing to work at their usual occupations in society, share a common interest in pursuing and practicing the teachings which Norbu Rinpoche continues to transmit.

The above information was largely extracted by John Reynolds from a biography in Tibetan appended to Professor Norbu's *gZi yi Phreng ba* (Dharmsala: Library of Tibetan Works and Archives, 1982).

Appendix Three

Commentary to the Plates

Plate 1

In this contemporary thanka, or painting traditionally done on cotton material so as to be easily rolled up for carrying, Garab Dorje, the first master of Dzogchen to manifest on this planet in this time cycle (born in the third century B.C.E.), appears in a luminous thigle of visionary light above Adzam Drugpa, one of the great Dzogchen masters of the late nineteenth and early twentieth centuries. Garab Dorje is here shown in the form of a Mahasiddha (a realized practitioner of tantra and/or Dzogchen), though he is also sometimes represented in a form similar to that used to depict the historical Buddha, Shakyamuni. Beside Garab Dorje (who is seated on a deerskin), is a tantric gourd, used to contain secret ritual objects, texts, etc. Adzam Drugpa is shown wearing the ordinary clothes of a Tibetan layman, with a fine formal silk robe over them, seated on his teaching cushion, ready to give teaching. On the small table in front of him are (left to right): a small damaru; bell and dorje; a melong or mirror used as a symbol to explain certain aspects of the teachings; and a skull cup offering bowl.

Plates 2 and 3

See captions.

Plate 4

Nubchen Sangye Yeshe was a great accomplished yogi, or Siddha, whose activities helped to ensure the survival and continuation of the teachings established in Tibet by Padmasambhava. During the period after Padmasambhava had left Tibet in which the Buddhist Dharma, after its initial spread, was suppressed for political reasons, it was virtually impossible for a community of monks to practice openly in the monasteries. The transmission and practice of the teachings was then carried forward by lay practitioners under the guidance of such masters as Nubchen Sangye Yeshe, who lived and practiced discreetly in lay communities in remote villages and mountain retreats far from the centres of political power. The teachings were thus preserved until the political climate once again became more favorable. Nubchen Sangye Yeshe was expert in controlling negative influences, and is shown in this detail wielding his purba to drive away demons. A yogi flies in the air above his cave, and the syllable *Hum*, symbol of the primordial state, manifests from a mountain.

Plate 5

In the teachings, energy as a general principle is regarded as feminine (active), while matter or substance is regarded as male (passive). Thus the class of beings that manifest as, or dominate certain aspects of, energy are considered feminine, and are called 'dakini' in Sanskrit, or 'khandro' (lit: 'space-goers') in Tibetan. There are both worldly and non-worldly dakinis. The non-worldly dakinis are classed in five groups, like the five Dhyani Buddhas, according to their type of activity. There are Sambhogakaya manifestations like Simhamukha (p. 57) and Vajrayogini, who are of the Buddha family, and as such are manifestations of the supreme activity of total realization; and Nirmanakaya manifestations such as Enlightened female teachers, realized consorts of the masters, and so on. Some dakinis manifest as Guardians, like Ekajati (p. 136). Then, among the worldly dakinis, there are 'flesh-eating dakinis or 'cannibal dakinis', and other kinds of dakinis who may harm human beings. In general, the dakinis may be of many kinds and may manifest in peaceful or wrathful, creative or destructive ways, some as human beings, and some as evil spirits.

Garab Dorje, during his lifetime on Earth, taught the dakinis for many years before he taught human beings. He prophesied that, of the beings who would realize the Dzogchen teachings, the majority would be female. Although this could mean that the number of women who would attain realization by applying the Dzogchen teachings would be greater than the number of men, it could also refer to the dakinis, whose number is far greater than that of human beings; moreover, hundreds of thousands of dakinis can have continuous contact with a master who has realized the Body of Light, whereas such contact is more difficult for ordinary human beings. Padmasambhava also taught many dakinis for four years after his miraculous birth near the Dhanakosha lake, and he is considered to be always surrounded by a court of them. The dakinis have thus come to be in charge of many teachings which have been entrusted to their care either by Padmasambhava himself, or by his consort Yeshe Tsogyal. dakinis, and the class of beings associated with watery places known as 'Nagas', guard a terma, or 'hidden treasure', until the time is ripe for its rediscovery and revelation by a *tertön*. Tertöns are reincarnations of the principal disciples of Padmasambhava, and other masters, who have particular connection with the eighteen various kinds of hidden treasures Padmasambhava decided to conceal for future generations. Padmasambhava lived in the ninth century C.E., and he prophesied that there would arise in the future three 'Grand', eight 'Great', twenty-one 'Powerful', 108 'Intermediate', and 1,000 'Subsidiary' tertöns of various kinds. Tertöns may reveal objects, substances, etc., or Dharma texts; in the latter case, the tertön needs visionary clarity, not only to find the texts, but also to interpret their meaning, as terma are often revealed in the language of the dakinis. Through the ongoing process of the discovery of terma the teachings have been continually renewed and refined as they have been passed on, instead of becoming less clear, or even lost altogether, as might have happened if only an oral transmission had existed.

Plate 6

Mandarava holds a vase of long life in her left hand. In her right hand she holds a *dadar*, a ritual arrow, whose straight shaft represents the life force of the individual as an active principle of the primordial state. Attached to the arrow shaft are: a *melong*, or mirror, which here, since it reflects everything, represents the all-encompassing nature of the primordial state; and five-coloured ribbons, whose fluttering represents the continual movement of the five elements which are carried on the prana, or life force, and enable the development and continual regeneration of the physical body to occur. Above Mandarava the dakinis of the five families bear offerings.

Plate 7

See captions.

Plate 8

Vairochana was one of the first seven Buddhist monks to be ordained in Tibet, receiving his vows from Shantarakshita. He was later requested by Padmasambhava and the king of Tibet, Trisong Deutsen, to go to Oddiyana to seek teachings there to bring back to Tibet. He set out on the journey accompanied by another Tibetan master, and when they reached Oddiyana they spent a long time with Shri Simha, a disciple of Manjushrimitra, Garab Dorje's principal disciple, who transmitted the Dzogchen Semde teachings to them. Vairochana's companion, satisfied with these teachings, then set out to return to Tibet, but died on the way. Vairochana remained in Oddiyana for another two years to receive further teachings from Shri Simha, and then returned to Tibet, where he was to give teachings to the King. Certain political factions at the court, however, sought to discredit Vairochana by claiming that the teachings he had brought back were invalid. By making false accusations against Vairochana that he had engaged in illicit relations with a wife of the King these factions managed to force Trisong Deutsen, against his will, to send the great master into exile in East Tibet for many years. But it so happened that in that part of east Tibet there was a local ruler who had a young son called Yudra Nyingpo. When this boy met Vairochana he was at once able to understand all the teachings Vairochana gave him. He also manifested many Dzogchen teachings from his own memory although he was too young ever to have studied them. Vairochana recognized him as the reincarnation of his companion on the journey to Oddiyana, and he became Vairochana's principal disciple, later also becoming a disciple of Padmasambhava. Vairochana ultimately regained favor with the King, when Vimalamitra convinced Trisong Deutsen that Vairochana's teachings were authentic, and Vairochana returned to the court, where together with Vimalamitra, Yeshe Tsogyal, and the King, he was instrumental in spreading the teachings throughout Tibet.

Plates 9 and 10

See captions.

Plate 11

The Fifth Dalai Lama's personal temple is known as Zongdag Lukang, and three walls of the murals it contains represent visions related to the Dzogchen teachings. One wall illustrates a commentary by Longchenpa on a Dzogchen tantra. called the *Rigpa Rangshar*, interpreted according to the Fifth Dalai Lama's own experience of practice, showing characteristic visions of the secret practice of Thödgal that leads to the realization of the Body of Light, or Rainbow Body. Another wall shows the eight manifestations of Padmasambhava and the eighty four principal Mahasiddhas of the tantric tradition. The third wall illustrates positions and movements of Yantra Yoga, a specifically Tibetan form of yoga. There are yantra yoga movements in the Tibetan indigenous Bön traditions, in the Buddhist Anuttarayoga and in the Inner tantras of the Nyingmapa, as well as in the teachings of Buddhist Dzogchen. These murals have never before been photographed because the temple is closed to the public by the authorities. The author managed to photograph them whilst revisiting Tibet in 1981, his first opportunity to visit his native land for more than twenty years.

Plates 12 and 13

The practical difference between Yantra Yoga and the Indian Hatha Yoga which is at present more widely known in the West is that Yantra Yoga works with a system of bodily movements linked to breathing, rather than with fixed positions, which are the basis of Hatha Yoga. The realizations aimed at are also fundamentally different in the two systems.

Plates 14-27

See captions.

Notes

1. My Birth, Early Life and Education, and How I Came to Meet My Principal Master

1 See Appendix 2 for a more detailed biography of the author.

2 The Chögyal (chos rgyal) was the reincarnation of the Shabdrung Ngawang Namgyel and was above the supreme monastic authority—the Je Khempo, elected by the two monastic colleges—and the supreme temporal ruler—the Deb or Desi, whose post was also elective.

2. An Introductory Perspective: the Dzogchen Teachings and the Culture of Tibet

1 For a full treatment of the significance of Bön in Tibetan culture, see: Namkhai Norbu, *The Necklace of Gzi, A Cultural History of Tibet*, published by the Information Office of His Holiness the Dalai Lama, Dharamsala, India, 1980; and also his more recent publication: *Drung, Deu, and Bön: Narrations, Symbolic Languages and the Bön Tradition in Ancient Tibet*, translated from Tibetan, edited and annotated by Adriano Clemente, (Library of Tibetan Works and Archives, 1995).

The root of the word 'Bon' means 'to recite', or 'chant', and so this name was applied to all those who recited mantras or performed rituals. Historically, one cannot properly speak of a single 'Bon religion', but only of a confluence of many streams of shamanic tradition. The fact that there is an etymological link betweeen the word bon and the Tibetan word for Tibet, bod, shows how deeply these traditions were identified with the area and rooted in it. Bon ritual practices work to enable the individual to go beyond dualism and to master the functioning of energy.

3. How My Master Changchub Dorje Showed Me the Real Meaning of Direct Introduction

1 The Tibetan year is arranged in a lunar calendar whose cycle most often begins with the New Moon in February. New Moon is from then on always the first of the month, and Full Moon corresponds to the 15th day. From a tantric point of view, the period of the waxing moon favors method, and therefore Heruka practices are done during this phase, within which the 10th day of the month is considered particularly auspicious, and is known as Padmasambhava's day, because the great master carried out very many actions on that day. The period of the waning moon, on the other hand, favors energy, and Dakini practices are thus carried out during this phase of the moon, with the 25th day known as Dakini day, being particularly auspicious. The 8th day of the month is dedicated to Tara and to Mahakala, while the 29th is dedicated to the Guardians of the teachings in general. The exception to the above rule is when, for astrological reasons, one of the days in question is regarded as inauspicious, since then its number is changed and the date does not correspond to the day in the lunar month.

The days of the week are the same as those in the Western calendar.

2 Bardo: in general use this term refers to the inter-mediate state that follows the death of the physical body and precedes the next rebirth.

More precisely there are six bardos: the three bardos that arise as phases of the progressive processes that occur between physical death and the next rebirth; and the bardo of birth (one's normal experience when one is awake rather than sleeping), the bardo of the dream state, and the bardo of *samadhi* or state of total concentration.

3 The Changchubsem Gompa, or 'Meditation on Bodhicitta', translated into English by Namkhai Norbu, Dr. Kennard Lipman and Barrie Simmons. Published by Shambhala Publications, Boston, Autumn 1986, under the title *Primordial Experience*; now (Fall 1999) unfortunately out of print.

4 Bodhisattva: someone who has committed him or herself to attain total realization for the benefit of all beings; the practitioner of Mahayana. The 'superior' or 'noble' *(arya)* Bodhisattva is the one who has already had access to Absolute Truth (from the first *bhumi* or third Path onwards).

5 Terma *(gTer-ma)* are texts or treasures hidden by *Padmasambhava* and Yeshe Tsogyal or other great masters of the past to be revealed at a given time. The treasures of Wisdom Mind *(dgongs-gter)* are revealed by some masters from the great clarity of their contemplation.

4. Dzogchen in Relation to the Various Levels of the Buddhist Path

1 See Namkhai Norbu: *Dzogchen and Zen*, Zhang Zhung Editions, Oakland, California, 1984, for a fuller treatment of this topic. Essentially the difference between Dzogchen and Zen is this: while the practitioner of Zen aims to realize a state of mind free of overvalued concepts, or a state of voidness (Tib: *mitogpa*), the practitioner of Dzogchen aims to go beyond this void state of mind to realize a state of pure primordial presence (Tib: *rigpa*) in which a total reintegration of the energy that is the continual manifest function of voidness can be accomplished. The understanding and a use of energy that are found in Dzogchen in practices such as Thödgal (which uses the 'rolpa' manifestation of energy as a means of rapidly uprooting dualism) and Yangthig are not found in Zen.

See also: Namkhai Norbu: The Way of Self-Liberation and the Great Perfection, edited by Elias Capriles; as yet unpublished.

2 The Tibetan term 'gyü' (rgyud) literally means 'woolen thread', and the image of the thread is intended to represent 'continuity'—the continual alternation of voidness and manifestation that is the Nature of our Base (see the following chapters for a full explanation of the Base, and the Nature). The Sanskrit term of which the Tibetan word 'gyü' is a translation is , and literally means 'the intricate pattern of weave of a woven fabric'. But the way the term is understood has become intimately connected with that of another Sanskrit term, prabandha, whose literal meaning is 'continuity'.

The image of a woolen thread, as in the term 'gyü', is used in relation to the Base to point out the way in which our experiences are strung in the continuity of the Base like beads strung along the thread of a rosary or mala. Just as between the beads of a rosary there are empty spaces in which there is only thread, so too, between each of our thoughts and our experiences, there are spaces; but, even though there is an empty space between them, and even though they are void—or empty—in themselves, thoughts and experiences nevertheless continue to manifest.

If we were to explain this example in terms of the three aspects of the Base (Essence, Nature, and Energy) as they are understood in the Dzogchen teachings we would say that the thread represents the Nature—which is the unbroken continuity of manifestation of the Essence (or voidness), while the beads represent the Energy.

Inside every bead (every thought or experience) in the example there is only thread (the continuity of emptiness' potentiality to manifest); and in our lives, even though each and every thought or experience is essentially empty, thoughts and experiences never stop arising.

While discussing continuity, it is perhaps worth adding here that the continuity between the Base, Path and Fruit is more integrated in Dzogchen than in the various levels of Tantra: we could even go so far as to say that, essentially, in Dzogchen, the Base is the primordial state, the Path is the primordial state, and the Fruit is the primordial state—and that there is thus a perfect continuity between them in that they all refer to the same thing: the true condition of the individual and the universe.

3 According to one of the histories of the origin of the *Guhyasamaja Tantra*, Shakyamuni Buddha himself transmitted tantric teachings to King Indrabodhi of Oddiyana (in Tibetan, King Ja). However, most tantric teachings—including the *Guhyasamaja Tantra*, according to some accounts—originally manifested to Nirmanakaya Mahasiddha through the Sambhogakaya.

4 Many Western translators mistakenly render *mahamudra* as 'great seal'. This error is the result of a wrong translation of the Tibetan composite word 'Chaggya Chenpo' *(phyag-rgya chen-po)*, which translates the Sanskrit *mahāmudrā*. The translators in question believe the 'gya' in *phyag-rgya* to be the same as the 'gya' that appears three times in the phrase *'samaya gya gya gya'* which is printed at the end of many terma *(gter-ma)* teachings of the Nyingmapa tradition in order to warn the reader that the teaching is very secret and he or she should not go around speaking about it. In this sense, 'gya' means 'sealed'. However, this is not the sense of the term in the composite term *phyag-rgya chen-po.* In the practice of Tantra, everything begins and ends with symbols. The manifestation of the divinities is in itself a symbol rather than the presence of a particular being, and the realization of the mahamudra means that one has totally integrated with this symbol so that there is only the symbol in question—a total symbol symbol: mahamudra.

5. With My Two Uncles Who Were Dzogchen Masters

1 For more information about the lifestyle of Tibetan Nomads, see Namkhai Norbu: 'A Journey into the Culture of Tibetan Nomads', Shang-Shung Editions, Merigar 58031 Arcidosso G.R. Italy, 1983.
As well as yogis who lived in caves, there were also nomadic yogis, called 'chadral' ('bya-'gral) who constantly moved from one place to another; they were not allowed to carry with them more than a few kilos of luggage and were not allowed to stay anywhere for more than very few days.

2 See *Machig Labrön* and the *Foundations of Chöd* by Jerome Edou, Snow Lion Publications, Ithaca, New York, 1996. And: *Women of Wisdom,* Tsultrim Allione, Routledge & Kegan Paul, London, 1984.

3 For a full account of the relationship between Milarepa (1040-1123) and his master Marpa (died 1098), see *The Life of Marpa the Translator* (trans. Nalanda Committee/ Chögyam Trungpa, Prajña Press, Boulder, 1982); *Tibet's Great Yogi Milarepa* (trans. Kazi Dawa Sangdup; ed. W.

Y. Evans-Wentz, Oxford University Press, London, 1928; rpt. 1969); and *The Hundred Thousand Songs of Milarepa* (trans. Garma C. C. Chang, Shambhala, Boulder, 1977).

6. The Base

1 All teachings have their own particular conception of the Base (the fundamental condition of the individual), the Path (the spiritual practice that must be done) and the Fruit (the state to be attained), all of which correspond to the characteristics of vehicle or teaching to which they belong. What is presented here is the Base, Path, and Fruit of Dzogchen.

2 The *Song of the Vajra* comes from the *Nyida Kajor*, the *Union of the Solar and Lunar Tantra*. It is also the principal mantra of the 'Bardo Thödrol', known in the West as the 'Tibetan Book of the Dead', and its syllables, in its original form, are in the language of Ogyen, or Oddiyana. The song is not a prayer, nor does the practice of it involve a visualization; rather it is to be sung in the state of contemplation, so that it may help the practitioner integrate his or her experience of the natural state with the level of energy through the sound of the song. Thus, in practice, the meaning of the Vajra Song is not as important as its sound.

3 'Ying' (Tibetan: *dbyings*). In the sense it is given here, this Tibetan term, which corresponds to the Sanskrit *dhatu,* is translated as 'dimension'. The *dharmadhatu,* the expanse or space of reality, is *chos-dbyings* in Tibetan; in Dzogchen reference is made to an 'internal ying' and an "external ying'.

4 The Tibetan term *khams,* which also corresponds to the Sanskrit *dhatu,* indicates the essence of the elements. The latter are called 'jungwa' *('byung-ba)* in Tibetan and *bhuta* in Sanskrit.

5 Katak (Tibetan *ka-dag*) or 'purity' characterizes the Dang form of manifestation of energy, whereas lhundrub *(lhun-grub)* or "self-perfectedness" characterizes the Rolpa and Tsal forms of manifestation of energy.

6 See: Giacomella Orofino: *Sacred Tibetan Teachings on Death and Liberation: Texts from the Most Ancient Traditions of Tibet,* Bridport, Dorset, UK (1990); *Death, Intermediate State and Rebirth in Tibetan Buddhism,* Lati Rinbochay and Jeffrey Hopkins, Rider, London, 1979; Namkhai Norbu's Italian translation of the Tibetan Book of the Dead: *Il Libro Tibetano dei Morti,* Namkhai Norbu, Newton Compton, Editori, Rome, 1983; and also: *The Tibetan Book of the Dead,* translated by Chögyam Trungpa and Francesca Freemantle, Shambhala Publications, Boulder, 1975.

It must be noted that, in the practices of the Dzogchen upadesha, or Mennagde, the correct perception of the Dang form of energy (corresponding to the dharmakaya), is the essence of the practice of Tregchöd; the correct perception of the Rolpa form of energy (corresponding to the sambhogakaya) is the essence of the practice of Thödgal, and the correct perception of the Tsal form of energy (corresponding to the nirmanakaya and to the condition called yermed, or 'inseparability') is the essence of the Fruit.

7. The Path

1 In this example the purity, clarity, and limpidity of the mirror itself represent the absolute condition—that which allows for the manifestation of all relative images, but which itself is not relative to anything; whereas the reflections that appear in the mirror—which lack substance and concreteness, and which are relative to every other reflection—represent the relative dimension and its illusory, apparitional character. So, in so far as the reflections are a function of the mirror (we could say they are the mirror's play of light and do not have existence except in the mirror), the relative *is*, in truth, the absolute.

2 See: *The Life and Teaching of Naropa*, H. V. Guenther, Oxford, 1963.

3 In the Mennagde there exist external, internal and even secret Ngöndro, but they are not compulsory preliminaries.

4 See *Clear Light of Bliss: Mahamudra in Vajrayana Buddhism*, Geshe Kelsang Gyatso, Wisdom Publications, London, 1982, p.126: "The practice with the action seal 'karmamudra' refers to the meditation with an actual consort. In order to practice with the action seal here at the completion stage you must already be familiar with causing your winds (subtle energies) to enter, abide, and dissolve in the central channel through the force of meditation. A person who cannot control the winds in this way through meditation cannot possibly do so through copulation. A lay practitioner who is currently unable to transform sexual activity into the path in this way should generate strong aspiration and motivation to be able to do so in future."

5 While commenting on the different descriptions of the system of channels for the circulation of subtle energy in different texts and practices, Chögyal Namkhai Norbu has explained that it does not have an 'objective' existence at the gross physical level, but that there is no doubt that it exists at the level of energy, because the practices that work with it produce verifiable effects. So the energy system will be visualized one way or another according to the effects sought. The Tibetan term *uma* is used to refer to the central channel when it is visualized beginning at the level of the navel, whereas when it is visualized as going down to the perineum, it is generally called *kundarma*.

6 See Namkhai Norbu, *Yantra Yoga. The Yoga of Movement*, Shang Zhung Editions Merigar. At present (1999) available only in Tibetan with English introduction, but translation into European languages is now nearing completion and it is intended that it will be published by Snow Lion Publications, Ithaca, New York. The book contains the root text of Vairochana, and a commentary by Namkhai Norbu.

7 Humkara was both a teacher and disciple of Padmasambhava.

8 See: *The Divine Madman: The Sublime Life and Songs of Drukpa Kunley*, translated by Keith Dowman, Rider, London, 1980.

9 This short biography of Ayu Khandro by the author is now published in *Women of Wisdom*, ed. Tsultrim Allione, Routledge & Kegan Paul, London, 1984.

8. The Fruit

1 In 'self-liberation observing the object' *(gcer-grol)*, by looking directly at the discursive, intuitive or super-subtle thought that is present at a given moment, what the thought is in truth—which is also what the mental subject looking at it is in truth—is recognized; in other words, the state of knowledge fully manifests. This has been compared to the recognition of an old friend, because what is thus recognized is one's own Essence. One recognizes one's own original face which precedes any form— something more intimate and more one's own than the most intimate of friends. This recognition is not the recognition of an object in terms of a concept or idea, but completely surpasses that type of recognition. It's not that one thinks to oneself: 'the thought or concept now presenting itself is nothing other than the true condition or the primordial nature of all existence', but that the mental subject disappears together with the thought that it had taken as an object. Since the duality of a subject and an object instantly disappears, together with the importance that we normally attribute to our experience, the tensions that normally tie up our existence are instantly cut, like the string tying a bundle of wood. As soon as this happens, the primordial state manifests in absolute relaxation. This mode or capacity of liberation is illustrated with the image of 'recognizing an old friend' in many Dzogchen texts, and is indicated by the words 'namtok no she pe drolwa' *(rnam-rtog ngo-shes-pas grol-ba)*.

2 This type or capacity of self-liberation (Shardrol, *shar-grol*) doesn't manifest through observing a thought or subtle concept that has already become established as an 'object' in relation to oneself as the observing subject: Shardrol is less intentional and more immediate than that. As the thought is arising and is about to become an object in relation to the perceiving

subject, there is a spontaneous movement of attention which dissolves in the self-liberation of whatever it was that was becoming established. In this case the self-liberation of delusion can't be compared to cutting the string that was tying a bundle of wood, because here the string which represents the tension inherent in the subject-object duality and in giving importance to one's experience breaks precisely in the moment it was being tied up. So perhaps a better example for this kind of self-liberation would be that of string tied with a knot that undoes itself as soon as the string is pulled. But it must be clear that in this case the knot undoes itself naturally rather than it being untied as the result of an intentional, self-conscious action. This mode or capacity of liberation, illustrated by the image of 'a snake that spontaneously undoes a knot in its own body', is indicated in many Dzogchen texts by the words 'namtok rangyi rangdrol' *(rnam-rtog rang-gis rang-grol).*

3 This is the self-liberation totally free from both action and reaction *(rang-grol),* which takes place in the very moment that any experience arises: whatever arises liberates itself as it arises, in the same way that a drawing made on water immediately disappears of its own accord. Neither an intentional action of the subject (as in Cherdrol), nor a spontaneous reaction of the subject (as in Shardrol), is required here. Whatever arises liberates itself of itself, without the need for anyone to do anything to liberate it. The string never begins to be tied up; voidness and appearances manifest coincidently. The practitioner is like the mirror which can freely reflect whatever presents itself, without the reflections in it either sticking to it or leaving any trace in it; the reflected image liberates in the very moment that it appears. Since there is no longer a mental subject that can be harmed by whatever manifests, it is said that at this stage the passions and whatever may arise are like a thief in an empty house. When one manifests this ultimate capacity of self-liberation, this is the realization of the Tregchöd *(khregs-chod).* This mode or capacity of liberation, illustrated with the image of a 'thief in an empty house', is indicated in many Dzogchen texts by the words 'namtok penme nömedu drolwa' *(rnam-rtog phan-med gnod-med-du grol-ba).*

4 In the Dzogchen teachings there are many explanations of the way in which samsara arises from the Base—understanding the Base as the undifferentiated experience from which both samsara and nirvana may actively arise. In such explanations, before the arising of objects as such, there arise both a 'disposition to perceive' and a 'self-preoccupation' which are the direct precedent of what later on will emerge as the mental subject.

5 The kind of realization that is attained as a result of the practice of the different Paths is not always the same: the nature of the Path that is followed will determine not only how rapidly the Fruit will be attained, but also what the nature of the Fruit will be.

6 Although, according to many texts of the Mahayana (an outstanding example being the *Vajracchedika Prajñāpāramitā Sutra* or *rDo rje gCod pa mDo)*, Enlightenment may only be attained at the end of three unmeasurable aeons, Ch'an or Zen Buddhism, which pertains to the Mahayana, affirms that its followers may attain Enlightenment in a single lifetime. However, this does not mean that Ch'an or Zen is the same as Dzogchen; the latter's understanding and use of energy is not shared either by Zen or by any other system of the Path of Renunciation, and no system of the Path of Renunciation or of the Path of Transformation leads to the levels of realization that constitute the ultimate Fruit of Dzogchen.

7 *Sambhoga* literally means 'enjoyment'. Chögyal Namkhai Norbu explains that the sambhogakaya has to do with the enjoyment of the wealth—unlimited in quality and in quantity—of the infinite manifestations of the potentiality of the rolpa aspect of the energy (or 'tukje') *(thugs rje)* of the individual's Base; these manifestations are enjoyed by our various senses. But, as Chögyal Namkhai Norbu cautions, in so far as 'enjoyment' on the physical level normally causes us to enter into thought, or mental judgment, followed in samsara by the development of attachment and aversion, it is perhaps better to render the term *sambhoga* as 'wealth'.

Appendix 2: Biographical Sketch of the Author

1 Kun-bzang Bro 'dul 'od gsal klong yangs rdo rje, 1898- .

2 sNang mdzod grub pa'i rdo rje, 1900- .

3 'Gro 'dul dpa' bo rdo rje, 1842-1924.

4 rDza dPal sprul Rin po che, O rgyan 'jigs med chos kyi dbang po, 1808-87.

5 During summer retreats he taught rDzogs chen and during winter retreats he taught *rtsa rlung*, the yoga of the channels and energies.

6 The term *rtogs ldan* means 'one who has attained understanding', and is more or less synonymous with *rnal 'byor pa*, a 'yogin'.

7 rGyal ba Karmapa, Rangbyung rig pa'i rdo rje, 1924-81.

8 Padma dbang mchog rgyal po, 1886-1952.

9 *thugs kyi sprul sku*

10 Ngag dbang rnam rgyal, 1594-1651.

11 Kun dga' dpal ldan, 1878-1950.

12 'Jam dbyangs chos kyi dbang phyug, 1910-73.

13 'Jam dbyangs blo gros rgya mtsho, 1902-52.

14 *dbang dang khrid*
15 *gzhung chen bcu gsum.* These texts are:
   (1) *Prātimokṣa sūtra*
   (2) *Vinaya sūtra* by Guṇaprabha
   (3) *Abhidharmasamuccaya* by Asaṅga
   (4) *Abhidharmakośa* by Vasubandhu
   (5) *Mūlamadhyamakakārikā* by Nagarjuna
   (6) *Madhyamakāvatāra* by Candrakirti
   (7) *Catuḥśataka* by Āryadeva
   (8) *Bodhicaryāvatāra* by Śantideva
   (9) *Abhisamayālaṃkāra* by Maitreya/Asaṅga
   (10) *Mahāyānasūtrālaṃkāra* by Maitreya/Asaṅga
   (11) *Madhyāntavibhāga* by Maitreya/Asaṅga
   (12) *Dharmadharmatāvibhāga* by Maitreya/Asaṅga
   (13) *Uttaratantra* by Maitreya/Asaṅga
16 gZhan phan chos kyi snang ba
17 *Dus 'khor 'grel chen*
18 *rGyud bzhi*
19 *rtsis dkar nag*
20 *gur brtag sam gsum*
21 Yongs 'dzin mchog sprul, Kun dga' grags pa, 1922- .
22 *rig gnas kyi skor*
23 rDzong gsar mkhyen brtse Rin po che, 'Jam mgon mkhyen sprul Chos kyi blo gros, 1896-1959.
24 *spyi ljon brtag gsum.* The *Hevajra Tantra* is also known as the *brtag gnyis* because it is divided into two parts.
25 *mun mtshams*
26 *dgongs gter*
27 Gangs dkar Rin po che, Karma bshad sprul Chos kyi seng ge, 1903-56.
28 *Na ro chos drug*
29 *rtsa ba'i bla ma*
30 Shar rdza bKra shis rgyal mtshan, 1859-1935.
31 *'ja 'lus pa*
32 *rdzogs chen 'dus sde*

Other Publications by Chögyal Namkhai Norbu

An Introduction to Dzogchen, Replies to Sixteen Questions. Shang Shung Edizioni, Merigar, 58031 Arcidosso, G.R., Italy, 1988.

A Journey into the Culture of Tibetan Nomads. Tibetan with English introduction. Shang-Shung Edizioni, Merigar, 58031 Arcidosso, G.R., Italy, 1983.

Dream Yoga and The Practice of Natural Light. Ed. M. Katz. Snow Lion Publications, Ithaca, New York, 1992.

Drung, Deu, and Bön: Narrations, Symbolic Languages and the Bön Tradition in Ancient Tibet. Library of Tibetan Works and Archives, Dharamsala, 1995.

Dzogchen and Zen. Ed. K. Lippman. Berkeley, 1984.

Dzogchen: The Self-Perfected State. Ed. A. Clemente. Penguin, London, 1989; Snow Lion Publications, Ithaca, New York, 1996.

Gangs ti se'i dkar chag, A Bonpo Story of the Sacred Mountain Ti-se and the Blue Lake Ma-pang. Rome, 1989.

Il Libro Tibetano Dei Morti. Translation into Italian of *The Tibetan Book of the Dead*. Newton Compton Editori, Rome, Italy, 1983.

Musical Tradition of the Tibetan People: Songs in dance measure. In Orientalia Romana. Rome, 1967.

On Birth and Life, A Treatise on Tibetan Medicine. Translated from Tibetan into Italian by Namkhai Norbu and Enrico Del'Angelo, and from Italian into English by Barry Simmons. Shang-Shung Edizioni, Merigar, 58031 Arcidosso, G.R., Italy, 1983.

"Some Observations on the Race and Language of Tibet." *Tibet Journal*, vol.7 n.3. Dharamsala,1982.

The Mirror: Advice on Presence and Awareness. Translated from the Tibetan by Adriano Clemente. Station Hill Press, Barrytown, 1996.

The Cycle of Day and Night: Where One Proceeds Along the Path of the Primordial Yoga. A basic text on the practice of Dzogchen, translated and edited by John M. Reynolds. Barrytown, 1979.

The Necklace of Gzi, A Cultural History of Tibet. Information Office of His Holiness the Dalai Lama, Dharamsala, India, 1981. Tibetan and English eds.

The Six Vajra Verses (Rigpai Kujyug). Ed. C. Goh. Singapore, 1990.

The Small Collection of Hidden Precepts. A Study of an Ancient Manuscript of Dzogchen from Tun-Huang, a study of a text by Buddhagupta, with a commentary by Namkhai Norbu, with an extensive glossary of Dzogchen terms. Shang-Shung Edizioni, Merigar, 58031 Arcidosso, G.R., Italy.

The Supreme Source (co-author A. Clemente). Snow Lion Publications, Ithaca, NY, 1999.

Primordial Experience: Manjushrimitra's Treatise on the Meaning of Bodhicitta in rDzogs chen. Namkhai Norbu with Kennard Lipman in collaboration with Barry Simmons. Translation from Tibetan into English. Shambhala Publications, Boston, 1983, 1986.

The Biography of A-Yu Khadro, Dorje Paldron. In *Women of Wisdom*, by Tsultrim Allione. London, 1984.

Yantra Yoga: The Yoga of Movement. Root text by Vairochana in Tibetan, with extensive commentary, in Tibetan, introduction in English. Shang-Shung Edizioni, Merigar, 58031 Arcidosso, G.R., Italy. (Translation into European languages in progress.)

Zer-Nga: The Five Principal Points: A Dzogchen Upadesha Practice. Shang-Shung Editions, London, 1985. (14D Chesterton Road, London, W10, England.)

Shang Shung Edizioni, Comunita Dzogchen, 58031 Arcidosso, G.R., Italy, publishes many books for practitioners by Chögyal Namkhai Norbu. Send s.a.e. for a list. E-mail: ssed@amiata.net

Some Publications by Chögyal Namkhai Norbu in Tibetan

Bod kyi lo rgyus 'phros pa'i gtam g.yung drung nor bu'i do shal. Dharamsala, 1981.

Bod rigs gzhon nu rnams la gros su 'debs pa gzi yi phreng ba. Dharamsala, 1982.

Byang 'brog gi lam yig. A Journey into the Culture of Tibetan Nomads. Arcidosso, 1983.

'Phrul 'khor nyi zla kha sbyor gyi dgongs 'grel dri med nor bu'i me long. Arcidosso, 1983.

sBab pa'i rgum chung. Arcidosso, 1983.

Bod sman stabs bder lag len byed tshul dngul gyi me long. Dharamsala, 1988.

Bod kyi ya thog gi lo rgyus skor, in *China Tibetology,* vol. 2, Beijing, 1988.

Bod kyi gna rabs dus rim gyi lo rgyus la zhib 'jug byed phyogs skor gyi bsam 'char phran bu, in *Bod ljongs zhin 'jug,* n. 3, Lhasa, 1988.

Bod ces bya ba'i tha snyad la dpyad pa, in *China Tibetology,* vol. 4, Beijing, 1989.

sGrung lde'u bon gsum gyi gtam e ma ho. Dharamsala, 1989.

Bod sman gyi cha lag skye ba dang 'tsho ba. Dharamsala, 1990.

Zhang bod gna rabs kyi lo rgyus nor bu'i me long. Sichuan, 1990.

rDzogs pa chen po'i skor gyi dris lan, in *China Tibetology,* vol. 3, Beijing, 1990.

The Dzogchen Community

Visit the Dzogchen Community Website at www.tashi.org

THE MIRROR: The Newspaper of the International Dzogchen Community.
   PO Box 227, Conway, Massachussetts 01341, USA
   Email: 102121.130@compuserve.com
   website: www.melong.com

INFORMATION ABOUT RETREATS conducted by Chögyal Namkhai
   Norbu in various parts of the world, and transcripts of tapes of some of
   his past retreats are available from:

EUROPE:
   Dzogchen Community in Europe: Merigar, 58031 Arcidosso, G.R., Italy.
   Tel: 39 0564 966837
   Email: merigar@amiata.net

NORTH AMERICA:
   Dzogchen Community in the USA: Tsegyelgar, PO Box 277, Conway,
      Massachusetts, 01341, USA
   Tel: 413 369 4153; Fax 413 369 4165
   Email: 74404.1141@compuserve.com
   Bookstore: tsegyalgarbookstore@yahoo.com

SOUTH AMERICA:
   Tashigar, Mariano Moreno 382
   5000 Cordoba, Argentina

RUSSIA:
   Dzogchen Community of Russia: Kunsangar: Tel: (095) 243-21156
   Email: kunsang@gar.dzogchen.art.ru

AUSTRALASIA:
   Dzogchen Community of Australia: Namgyalgar, PO Box 14, Central
      Tilba, NSW 2546.
   Phone/fax: 61.2.4476 3446
      Email: namgyal@acr.net.au

Index